Naomi E. Lane
4438 Marguerite St.
Vancouver, B.C.
V6J 4G6

Naomi E. Lane
4438 Marguerite St.
Vancouver, B.C.
V6J 4G6

THE PASSION FOR
FASHION

THE PASSION FOR
FASHION

ADRIAN BAILEY

Photographs by

PIERS BIZONY & RICHARD VANSPALL

PREFACE

This book is a survey of the changing fashions in dress over the past three centuries, since the time when fashions were more or less liberated from the hierarchy of Court costumes, until the mid 1950s when fashion began to move away from mainstream traditions of couture to the more free-style 'street clothes' of today.

I have avoided making the book a catalogue of costume—there are many excellent reference works of this kind—but have chosen to concentrate on the cycles of fashion and developments in women's clothes, with a brief look at men's attire, since the former is more affected by art movements and the rise of prosperity, and the so-called 'zeitgeist', or spirit of the age.

The book took a fair amount of organization, especially in the photography, and I am indebted to the valuable work of Piers Bizony and Richard Vanspall of the Longroom Studio. I would also like to thank John Woodcock for his charming drawings that decorate the chapter headings; Francesca Edgar who applied make-up with skill and historical knowledge; Judith Robertson, who designed the book and also acted as Wardrobe Mistress and Caterer Extraordinary—assisted by Jackie Kay—while on location; the staff of Angel Morris who took such trouble to provide the correct costumes and accessories with enduring patience and advice; Madeleine Ginsburg and the staff of the Costume & Textile Department of the Victoria and Albert Museum; also the curators of the Geffrye Museum and Transport Museum in London; the American Museum in Bath, and Clandon Park in Surrey. I am grateful for the untiring efforts of Anne Marie Ehrlich for picture research; the publisher Hubert Schaafsma who purchased a wide and generous selection of fashion plates from the Doris Langley-Moore Collection in order that this book would have abundant illustrative material; to Pippa Rubenstein whose administrative skills and helpful suggestions smoothed the way ahead; and finally to Angela Royston, who, with Jenny Sharman's help, edited the text night and day, at weekends, through epidemics of influenza, and cut verbose passages with the skill of a couturier shaping fabric.

Art Editor   Judith Robertson
Editor   Angela Royston
Commissioning Editor   Pippa Rubinstein

Dragon's World Ltd
Limpsfield
Surrey RH8 0DY
Great Britain

© Dragon's World Ltd 1988
© Text and drawings Adrian Bailey 1988

British Library Cataloguing in Publication Data

Bailey, Adrian
    A passion for fashion : changing styles
    in dress from 1700–1950.
    1.   Western costume, 1700–1950
    I.   Title
    391'.009
    ISBN 1 85028 063 0
Typesetting by Florencetype Limited,
Kewstoke, Avon
Printed in Spain by SIRVEN GRAFIC, S.A.
D.L. B-37.447-88.

CONTENTS

Chapter 1

CYCLES OF CHANGE

Fashion, which has become an intrinsic feature of our society, began more or less in the eighteenth century on any significant scale, and was an expression of wealth through industry. Money spent on clothes, once the privilege of the few, became the expectation of the many. Men's fashions were muted and sincere, a reflection of their professional status and judgement, but a measure of their success was apparent in the clothes chosen by their wives—what his wife wore was a reflection of a man's achievement—while an unmarried girl dressed in accordance with the expectations of the society to which she belonged. And so fashion found its main creative outlet in women's clothes. As for the children, their clothes were, in the main, scaled-down versions of styles worn by adults. Fashion was found, too, to possess its own dynamism with recurring cycles of change. It also responded to the spirit of the age, the mood of the times and the direction which society was taking. This book traces, in the following chapters, the many stages and developments of that phenomenon we call fashion—a passion with some, a necessity for most people, and something that few of us can easily ignore.

The Schloss Belvedere, Vienna, in 1785. The figures are wearing fashionable morning dress influenced, of course, by the current styles of Paris, and include the robe à l'anglaise *and the* polonaise, *seen practically everywhere. Ladies are carrying fans and parasols, and one has her hands in the pockets of her dress.*

Whether we like it or not, we are all involved in fashion, in one way or another. The clothes that we wear, our shoes, our hats and other accessories, indicate our class and nationality, and can date us to within a decade or sometimes to within a year or even a brief season, such is the rapid rate of change in dress. Most people follow the styles of contemporary fashions either because they wish to avoid being singled out—a lady in the eighteenth century, quoted later in this book, said, 'I don't want to be pointed out in the street'—or because, to be noticed is precisely their intention. They desire to be leaders of fashion, to be *avant-garde*, and to be seen to be adventurous or discriminating.

What is it all about? What is the purpose or meaning of fashion, if anything? Fashion in clothes is one of the prime expressions of a mainly youthful emergent class or group in our society, the clothes nourishing the ego of the individual, while confirming and celebrating the group's social or professional status, or both. This is the sociologists' view, or one of their views. Economists hold different but not unrelated theories, pointing out how the fashion magazines, and those that advertise in them, conspire with textile manufacturers and cosmetic companies to create a healthy market of demand and supply, supported by the fantasy created by fashion journalists and photographers.

In the background are the creators of styles, the dress designers and couturiers, the 'tyrants' of fashion, who now and then seem to take leave of their senses, dropping a hemline, lowering a neckline, or pinching a waistline to the delight of some and the consternation of others, especially the volatile garment industry that has to watch very closely the current trends to anticipate a sudden demand and have the clothes ready.

But all this is rather arid stuff, for statistics and economists' theories cannot explain the passion for fashion of those among us who, quite simply, love clothes and the accessories of costume for their own sake, and for that special rapport that the fashion-conscious person may feel for a particular designer, or colour, or style, garment, shoe, hat, bracelet, what you will. There are those with a natural gift for taste in clothes who can see at a glance what a suit, a dress, shoe or hat will do for them. Those, in short, who know a good thing when they see it.

The spell cast by fashion has remained undiminished, from the excesses of Marie Antoinette two centuries ago, to the lady who recently admitted to owning over two hundred pairs of shoes with matching handbags, and wardrobes crammed with suits and dresses, many of which had never been worn, nor were likely to be since she bought, on average, one complete outfit every week! Fashion is one of the more rewarding expressions of a vigorous consumer society, that is, a society that demands and finds stimulus in variety and constant change. Fashion in clothes, as in cars, electronics, household appliances, and other goods, reflects economic growth and social progress.

Fashion may be an indication of the developing role of the sexes in society and their relationship to each other. The short skirts, short hairstyles and boyish looks of the Twenties demonstrated women's emancipation, while the increasing equality of the sexes and reversal of roles may have produced the current unisex styles, and the uniformity of sweaters and jeans. I am speaking here of the fashions of democratic societies of the Western consumer nations we call 'modern', where the inexorable march forward seems inevitable.

Mantua 1690

Robe battante 1700

Piedmontese (1770)

Robe à la française 1750
or sacque dress

Robe à l'anglaise 1770

Relevée 1773

Robe à la polonaise 1778

Robe à la créole or *en gaulle* 1780

'*A l'anglaise*' with
pierrot jacket 1788

Empire line 1800

1816

1829

1839

Crinoline 1859

First bustle 1868

Cuirasse bodice 1876

Second bustle 1881

Gibson girl 1890

1914

1923

1927

1933

The changing shape of women's fashions from the end of the seventeenth century shows the development from the trained mantua through the various robes, and the chemise dress, to the bell-shaped crinoline, the back-fullness bustle, and finally the tubular or linear style that, give or take a few brief departures such as Dior's New Look of the late 1940s, is still with us today.

Plus ça change . . . the puffed sleeves, swept-up hat with plumes and full-skirted dress of 1836 are echoed after sixty years by fin de siècle *fashions, OPPOSITE. Both periods of style felt the need to emphasize the narrow waist by means of wide shoulders and a full skirt.*

Evening Dress.

A constant state of flux

It may be useful here to differentiate between the terms costume and dress, style and fashion. Costume is clothing which represents a particular period or place, or which is traditionally worn by those in certain social positions. We speak of national costume, Court costume, and theatrical costume. Dress is our everyday apparel, and subject to the sway of fashion, yet some types of dress can be unchanging, such as formal evening dress or mourning dress.

Style is more individual, fashion more collective and dependent on current trends. Style is that personal flair for wearing clothes with elegance and confidence, although one can speak of a fashion *style* or mode. Madame de Staël, the eighteenth century French essayist and leader of Paris salons, had great personal style, but she was famously unfashionable.

Fashion's power stems from its ability to nourish the egos of its many adherents, confirming their sense of taste and, more importantly, their sense of timing. Fashion is self-enhancing without necessarily being flattering. To be in fashion is to be ahead of the game, or at least in the leading pack. That is why it is in a constant state of flux—the supply is created by the demand, the demand encouraged by the capricious whims of supply, impelled by novelty. But as the editor of a French fashion magazine said recently, 'Fashion moves in ever-decreasing circles, for there is nothing new under the sun. What may be perceived as new is a contemporary interpretation of what is old.'

The phenomenon of fashion, as we shall see in later chapters, seems to possess its own autonomy and dynamic power: if a hemline is to rise, or a neckline to plunge, then it will do so. The question frequently asked, and never satisfactorily answered, is whether or not fashions are created solely by designers, or whether the designers anticipate what is about to occur anyway, with a certain gift for prescience. Do fashions arrive spontaneously and independently of outside influences?

Cynical observers of fashion trends have suggested that designers survive only according to their ability to follow the precept: 'Look to see where the people are going, and lead them where they drive you.' Various theories about fashion trends have

The exaggerated gigot sleeves of 1894 made a brief come-back, in a less pronounced style, in 1934—a gap of forty years. Fashions recur because designers are hard pressed to think of anything radically new. The child wears a lace, pelerine-type collar, the butterfly bows and ribbon streamers being common features of the time.

13

been propounded, such as that of the 'shifting erogenous zone', where fashions selectively emphasize various erotic zones of the female body in turn. Clothes may reveal an erotic element that can be overtly sexually provocative, or subtly so, depending on the social attitudes of the times. Thus there were periods in history when naked breasts caused little comment, but the glimpse of an ankle caused offence. As the historian Willett Cunnington put it, 'Woman is perpetually experimenting with her body to see whether various bits of it can be exposed with success.'

The thirty-year cycle of change

Perhaps the most thorough contribution on the autonomy of fashion came from the work of the generally overlooked American writer Agnes Brooks Young, whose book *The Recurring Cycles of Fashion*, published in 1937, was the outcome of painstaking research involving the tracing of eight thousand carefully chosen fashion plates of day dresses, in order to establish the immutable cycles of change. She chose day dresses, rather than evening wear or sports clothes, because they are more representative of mainstream fashions. The cycle appeared not to affect men's clothes, but only the basic skirt and sleeve shapes of women's clothes, such as the bell-shape of the crinoline, and the back-fullness of the bustle, which appeared to come and go of their own accord.

Young's work included a plate for every year from 1760 until 1937, and is a valuable source of reference for fashion changes, showing the cyclic progress from the bell shape to the back-fullness to the tubular shape, and back again to the bell shape. In fact, when Young's book was published, the tubular style was still in fashion. The change to the bell shape was overdue, and was not to be fully realized until Christian Dior's 'New Look' of 1947, although the change over was supposed to occur every thirty years or so. 'The evidence seems to indicate,' said Young, 'that the fundamental and durable changes that are embodied in fashion cycles are independent of historic events, of epochs of thought and ideals, and of artistic periods, though some of these things may occasionally leave a trace on dress.'

Yet Agnes Young ignores the effect that epochs of thought, and in particular art movements such as the rococo, romantic and neoclassic styles had on dress. The late James Laver, leading authority and expert on the subject of costume and fashion, maintained that fashion reflected the age or epoch, but confirmed Young's observations of the thirty-year cycle, pointing out the 'curious psychological fact that it is impossible to admire any fashion again until it is thirty years old, that is, until a whole generation has elapsed.'

Laver proposed a table of responses to fashion in his book *Taste and Fashion*, published in the same year as Agnes Young's book. Clothes, Laver claimed, are thought indecent ten years before their time, daring a year before, smart when in fashion, dowdy a year later, hideous after ten years, ridiculous after twenty, amusing, and presumably acceptable, after thirty years, and so on, until after a century the style is thought romantic. This fashion 'law' is now decidedly obsolete, since the miniskirt returned after fifteen years.

A fashionable, full day dress as worn in Paris in 1789, according to the Lady's Magazine. *The dress was probably worn only in the afternoon, since it must have taken the entire morning—assisted by maids and hairdressers—to arrange. Never again would fashions be so elaborate, encumbering and downright eccentric.*

The right place at the right time

Fashions also respond to what has been called the '*zeitgeist*', or spirit of the age, a theory offered by the historian Max von Boehn, which suggests that the social climate has an effect upon, among other things, art and fashion. If the spirit of the age leans towards the romantic, as it did throughout Europe in the first half of the nineteenth century, romanticism is powerfully revealed in art, literature, poetry, architecture and, to a certain extent, in fashions. Thus the Grecian modes of 1800 were inspired by the neoclassic movement, the frills, bonnets and bows of the 1820s to the 1850s reflected the sentimentality of the romantic style, while the clothes of the mid Victorians were both formal and demanding, representing perhaps the strength and solidity of that society, its rules and manners, collective self-esteem and powerful economy. Today, the challenging of traditional values has created clothes which in themselves challenge and show contempt for traditions and for social ideals.

The spirit of the age, the 'feeling in the air', also gives rise to new fashions in tune with that feeling, and provides the opportunity for a new designer to reveal his or her talents and prescience—a designer who has arrived in the right place at the right time. Hence the appearance of the first couturiers such as Worth, Paquin, Poiret and Chanel. Fashion has proved a splendid vehicle for commercial exploitation of a people eager to accept and acknowledge the slightest change, and the most outrageous dictates of style from the couturiers. But fashion is a preoccupation of many and a force not to be underestimated. 'Society,' said Thomas Carlyle, the author of *Sartor Resartus*, the first serious study of fashion as a social phenomenon, 'which the more I think of it astonishes me all the more, is founded upon cloth.'

Boudin's charming painting 'The Beach at Trouville', 1863, records the morning promenade of the Empress Eugénie and her party, on a windy day. It is likely that everyone was wearing dresses by Worth, the Englishman who became the first couturier, and Court dressmaker, in 1860.

15

Chapter 2

COSTUMES OF POWER
1670-1790

For most of the eighteenth century, fashions were shaped by the royal Courts of Europe, especially the Court at Versailles, where tastes were swayed by the two *grandes dames* of fashion, the Marquise de Pompadour, and Queen Marie Antoinette. Only the wealthy could afford to be fashionable anyway, and the division between privilege and poverty was strictly defined by sumptuary laws, or by wealth: your status was shown by whether you could afford a wig—unless you had stolen it.

The French were, as always, the leaders of fashion, but it was in London that the commercialization of fashion began, when England's capital was 'the shop window of Europe' and English inventions mechanized the textile industry. It was during this century, the 'Age of Enlightenment' that the precursors of our modern attire appeared in France—the mantua and sack dresses worn by women, and the three-piece suit adopted by men, the suit gradually acquiring the sombre overtones of commerce.

*N*ever before in France, certainly never since Charlemagne, was there such grandeur, such magnificence, such absolute power, as that enjoyed by Louis XIV, and the Court at the Palace of Versailles. Louis saw himself occupying a station only marginally lower than that of God, and on being defeated in battle by the Duke of Marlborough in 1704, he is said to have complained petulantly, 'God seems to have forgotten all I have done for for Him.'

Pictures of the Sun King in all his glory, and the 'terrifying majesty of bearing that came so naturally to him', show Louis attired in an opulent costume that could not possibly be matched by his nobles and courtiers. Fashion was imprisoned in the stiff brocades, heavy silks and ruffles of Court costume—*Le Grand Habit*—but only the right hand of the Almighty on Earth could wear a coat stitched with enough gold thread to stretch from Versailles to Paris, and a robe weighted down with diamonds that reputedly cost over £12,000,000, equal perhaps to the cost of a war, or at least a full-scale military campaign.

Such a display was not merely intended to reinforce Louis' boundless self-esteem, but to emphasize his Divine Right. Only the King's mistress could wear clothes of equal finery. It was not fashion as we understand it today, but the costume of power and privilege. Of the European monarchs, only Elizabeth I seems to have equalled Louis' pomp and glory.

'She wore ruffs and lace of almost unbelievable complexity, her hair elaborately adorned with pearls and jewels, her vast ornate dresses alive with rubies, sapphires and diamonds. And nor were these clothes kept for portraits only: so bedecked, she was carried in a litter through London and through the countryside on her famous progresses, like some monstrous painted but living idol . . . the cost was prodigious, for gods and goddesses must never appear old-fashioned and their clothes always had to be radiant and new.'

The King's new clothes were decidedly the height of fashion—they were undeniably exclusive—and both Louis and Elizabeth were 'fashion conscious' spending a great deal of time on their personal appearance, favouring only the most sumptuous silks, lace and brocades. Louis was a stickler for formality and tradition, which weighed heavily on the free spirit of fashion.

Wigs and furs – The symbols of status

In the seventeenth and early eighteenth centuries, few could afford to be fashionably dressed, and the gulf between the rich and the poor was reassuringly unbridgable, while that between the very rich and the country squire was only relatively less wide and reinforced by sumptuary laws. These laws restricted or prohibited the wearing of certain garments. They have throughout history been designed to maintain a strict social hierarchy, or to protect trade interests. Fernand Braudel, in *Capitalism and Material Life*, argues that 'Subject to incessant change, costume everywhere is a persistent reminder of social position. The sumptuary laws, therefore, expressed the wisdom of governments, but even more the anger of the upper classes when they saw the *nouveaux riches* imitate them.'

When fashion ruled. No one dared aspire to such splendour as displayed by the monarch. In this miniature painting, after Isaac Oliver, about 1580, Elizabeth I wears the ruff which was itself a symbol of privilege. A visitor to England noted that the Court had 'splendid silken stuffs and nothing is too expensive for them; the ladies especially look very clean with their linen and ruffs all starched in blue.'

Fur, for example, was thought too good for the common people. It gave them airs and graces beyond their station. In thirteenth-century France, Philippe le Bel passed a law forbidding the use of vair (squirrel fur) or *petit gris* (Russian squirrel fur) except by him and his peers. Fur was singled out for this form of legislation because it was the only status-conferring type of apparel around; elaborate fabrics and jewellery had not been developed sufficiently to be status symbols and to be functional and fashionable as well.

In London, the City sheriffs attempted to stop women from trimming their hoods with fur other than lambswool or rabbit because, 'servants and women of loose life, bedizen themselves,

English Court dress of the 1790s followed the tradition of large, hooped petticoats. The bodice was tight-waisted, and a long train was attached to the waist. Head-dress was the obligatory ostrich feathers with a turban or tiara. Jewels adorned the powdered coiffure *from which streamers of lace, known as lappets, were suspended. On the ascendancy of George IV in 1820, hoops were abolished but the feathers, train and gloves were retained.*

19

An early eighteenth century
robe manteau, robe battante *or*
'Adrienne', the domestic 'undress' of
Society. Since by today's standards
the figure in this engraving appears
overdressed, the term may be
misleading. 'Undress' simply meant
the wearer was not attired for formal
or ceremonial occasions for which
Court dress would be worn.

and wear hoods furred with *gros vair* and with miniver, in the guise of good ladies.' In fact, the sumptuary laws had little effect even though the punishment could be severe—life imprisonment was imposed on importers of Indian cotton in eighteenth-century France when legislation attempted to protect the French textile industry. Even the threat of the guillotine would not have deterred women in their urge to be fashionable. 'All the ladies are again wearing robes of Indian cotton,' reported a shocked observer, 'although this has been so often prohibited.' Women have always been refreshingly indifferent to petty laws made by men.

The introduction of the wig in France may have been a further measure to emphasize social status and widen the class gap in seventeenth-century France. Louis XIV is said to have commanded the services of 42 wigmakers, and to have changed his wigs several times a day. False hair and wigs had been employed since Roman times. According to Richard Corson's *Fashions in Hair*, the wig was introduced into France by Louis XIII when, in 1624, he started to lose his hair. The wearing of wigs had long been associated first with loss of hair—Louis XIV took to wearing a wig for this reason in the 1650s—and then with disguising grey hair, a measure adopted by Charles II. Once the monarch had introduced wigs they became a vogue which everyone else was duty bound to follow. Eventually, wigs became a useful indicator of status: 'Wigs came as a broad mark to distinguish rich and poor', stated *Chambers Journal*, 'and though beginning only at the price of £2 or £3, they soon rose to £50, and were indeed a formidable class barrier.' Such was the value of large and elaborate wigs that the fine art of wig-snatching was commonplace, the technique not unlike the current method in Italy of bag-snatching by motor-scooter. In the seventeenth and eighteenth centuries, a dog (or sometimes a small boy), perching on the thief's shoulders, was at just the right level to snap up the victim's wig before making a quick getaway.

Fashion has always been linked to wealth and a healthy economy. According to Agnes Brooks Young, it is not affected by fluctuations in the economy, not even by wars. During the Siege of Paris in 1870 fashion bulletins were despatched to the outside world by balloon! But before the consumer revolution of the late eighteenth century, fashions were slow to change. The high hairstyles of the 1700s, known as the *fontange*, were in fashion for ten years, and although the King detested them, even he could not do anything about them. Eventually the arrival at Court of the neatly *coiffured* Lady Sandwich brought styles toppling down.

Finesse and frivolity – French domination of fashion

The French aristocracy and professional classes created and maintained the *status quo*, as they had done for centuries, and for centuries they influenced Western society, even the insular English – as the testimony of Van Meteren, Dutch Consul to England in the reign of Elizabeth I, shows. He found that the English dressed in 'elegant, light and costly garments, and changed their fashions every year, both men and women'.

Before the first fashion plates appeared in magazines at the end of the eighteenth century, French fashions were broadcast through the agency of dolls, attired in the latest mode. There is some controversy as to the authenticity of several surviving dolls, or mannequins, principally because they are too small – the true fashion doll was at least half-size and most were fully life-size so that the dress in which the doll was sent could later be sold by the recipient, usually a dressmaker.

There is no doubt, though, that the dolls did exist and were known variously as 'Pandoras', 'Jointed Babies', 'French Babies', '*Mademoiselles*' and 'Fashion Babies', the bodies were made in Germany, the heads and clothes in France, and the whole figure assembled in Paris. Such figures had been despatched from France since at least the fifteenth century, from one royal Court to another to show the latest Court fashions. In *The Collector's Book of Dolls* the authors (the Colemans) say that 'Dolls had a very important part in disseminating knowledge of changing fashion styles. During the eighteenth century great fashion dictators . . . used dolls to show current fashions.' The 'Great Dictator' the Colemans had in mind was Rose Bertin, dressmaker to Marie Antoinette who, if not great, was certainly influential and decidedly extravagant.

These famous dolls, called 'Lord and Lady Clapham', from London's Victoria and Albert Museum are not, strictly speaking, fashion dolls, but they show remarkable details of the contemporary attire of the late seventeenth century.

A simple sacque *dress, or* robe à la française, *the most popular dress of the eighteenth century. Some gowns and robes, until about 1750, were worn closed with a wrap-over bodice extending and joined to a wrap-over skirt. Here, the lady wears an open gown with a simple lace cap on her powdered wig. The silk face patches were fashionable throughout the century.*

In January 1712, one such Pandora arrived at the Covent Garden milliner's shop of Charlotte Wood, who signed herself 'Betty Cross-Stitch', and seems to have been long overdue. In a letter to Addison and Steele's *The Spectator* a lady wrote, 'I was almost in Despair of ever more seeing a Model, when last *Sunday* I overheard a lady, in the next pew to me, whisper another, that at the *Seven Stars* in *King-Street Covent-Garden* there was a *Mademoiselle* compleatly dressed just come from *Paris.*' The dress met with the lady's approval. 'The Mantua has no Leads in the Sleeves, and I hope that we are not lighter than the *French* Ladies, so as to want that kind of Ballast; the Petticoat has no Whalebone, but sets with an Air altogether galant and *dégagé*; the *Coiffure* is inexpressibly pretty, and in short, the whole Dress has a thousand Beauties in it, which I would not have as yet made too publick.'

The fashion leaders of the French Court, the true arbiters of taste, were usually the mistresses of the King, at least until Queen Marie Antoinette arrived. Everyone else took their cue from the top, although the reactionary Duchesse d'Orleans complained that there was no regulation of fashion: 'Tailors, all those who make dresses, and hairdressers, invent them to please themselves.'

'The most ludicrous fashion'—
Fads and formality at Court

In the Court, with its finely structured hierarchy, the forces of fashion as described by such theorists as Georg Simmel, Herbert Spencer and the economist Thorstein Veblen, arose from competitiveness and the need to maintain a rigid class structure. 'Fashion is basically an emulation of prestige groups,' claims Simmel or, as William Hazlitt put it, 'Gentility fleeing from vulgarity.' Court etiquette could be decidedly contradictory and you had to know the rules—to imitate or not to imitate, that was the question. When Louis XIV shaved off his moustache in 1680, it was expected that those gentlemen at Court, who wore moustaches, would follow the King's lead. Similarly, when Marie Antoinette lost her hair after her confinement, at a time when hair styles were higher and more eccentric than ever before, the ladies of the Court moderated their *coiffures* in deference to the Queen's misfortune.

For these women of the Court, their positions insecure, their futures unpredictable and subject to the whims of the King, fashion and their day-to-day appearance was a safe refuge and preoccupation. Furthermore, time hung heavily, and a thousand palace clocks measured off the long hours. Relationships were fragile, gossip rife, and fashion a game played in earnest. It was not easy, though, to impose a fashion change on a formally regulated Court costume. Hairstyles were one way.

'Madame the Duchesse de Nevers came in with her hair dressed in the most ludicrous fashion,' wrote Madame de Sevigné, cattily, in 1671, when the Court hairdresser, La Martin, had created a new style. 'My dear, it is the most ridiculous sight you can imagine.' But her disapproval was short-lived. 'Now La Martin is spreading the fashion . . . I saw yesterday the Duchesse de Sully and the Comtesse de Guiche; their heads are charming. I give in.' They were still at it seventy years later. Apparently, Madame de Pompadour had 'a hundred entrancing ways of arranging her hair—now powdered, now in all its silken glory, now brushed straight back, ears showing, now in curls on her neck . . . till the Court went nearly mad attempting to imitate her inimitable *coiffures*.'

Court life became relatively more relaxed after the death of the inflexible Louis XIV in 1715, but even the moderate Louis XV, when he came of age, demanded much the same Court formality and etiquette. Court costume, *Le Grand Habit*, was a close-fitting bodice with a heavily-boned canvas lining, short sleeves and an off-the-shoulder neckline, with a petticoat and long train. Stiff, under-petticoats were worn, and under them wire paniers to form a wide, kidney-shaped skirt. Fabrics were lavishly decorated with gold and silver embroidery, set with gemstones, and garments were secured by jewelled clasps. Such was the weight of clothing

Ladies of the Court of Louis XIV, in the latter part of the seventeenth century, wore their hair piled high in a tour *over a wire frame or* commode. *The style was known as the* 'fontange'. *The term also applied to a fan-like lace and linen cap with trailing lappets of ribbon.*

23

THE PASSION FOR FASHION

The robe à l'anglaise, *a development of the mantua, appeared about 1770. It was pleated down the back to the waist, without a waist seam, and was known as the fourreau style. As the style developed, the seams were gathered in close to the small of the back extending to a point below the waist.*

and jewellery worn at Court that exhausted ladies required regular periods of rest to recover their strength and composure.

Court dress, for men as for women, was made of rich silks from Lyon and Italian brocades, satins and exquisite laces, and were entirely the expression of wealth and privilege. With the steady democratization that occurred throughout the eighteenth century, wealth from trade was distributed throughout the lower echelons of society with the result that fashions were tempered by the common touch.

The mantua — New Look of the eighteenth century

Men's clothes in particular were influenced by the demands of trade and the pursuit of commerce. There would be little scope, in this lifestyle, for the peacock vanity of silk and satin previously worn throughout the seventeenth century. Gradually, the formal elegance and silken dalliance would be replaced by a more utilitarian style, and eventually by the woollen fabric of the Victorian age, when the luxury of individuality had to be sacrificed to uniformity and corporate power.

The two most significant and fundamental changes in menswear occurred when the doublet and hose—the bodice and short, stuffed breeches that had been worn by men since at least the fourteenth century—finally gave way to the suit (the coat, waistcoat and breeches), sometime about the 1650s. In fashion terms it was not before time, since the style had lasted over three hundred years.

Women's clothes also underwent a marked change. The formal dresses with heavily boned bodices, worn with a trained skirt, were gradually superseded by lighter, looser garments that had their origins in the robes worn informally in the house—loose, full morning gowns that had been popular for at least a hundred years. These morning or dressing gowns—in France called the *robes de chambre*—perhaps derived from a T-shaped garment influenced by the oriental kimono or caftan of richly embroidered silk, featuring half-sleeves to below the elbow.

Throughout the sixteenth and seventeenth centuries women had worn bodices and petticoats with an over-mantle opened in front to show the petticoat, which might be in a contrasting or matching material. Now, in the early eighteenth century, the bodice was being replaced by a corset or stays, while the petticoat remained, and the over-mantle was given greater prominence as the principal part of the ensemble. In fact, it was the forerunner of modern dress. The open front of the gown had the edge, where it fell to the floor, lifted up and back, to be bunched or folded over the rump where it was attached by tapes or cords to two buttons.

The robe included a train, folded upwards to join the gathered and fastened superfluous material. This created a back-fullness profile (to be repeated in the 1770s and 1870s with similar details). The entire ensemble was called the mantua, probably from the French *manteau*.

During the latter part of the seventeenth century, and the earlier part of the eighteenth, the loose mantua began to take on more the shape of the body beneath it. The robe developed into a day dress for social engagements. It was never boned, but stays were worn underneath to maintain an upright carriage (even children had to wear stays, boys and girls alike, to impose the desired body posture and also as a measure of discipline). The gown was pleated at the shoulder, around the waist and over the hips. There were two wide pleats each side of the centre back, and these followed over the shoulders, one each side, and down the front of the gown to the waist.

The visible part of the stays, was faced with a decorated panel, the stomacher, and bore a series of bows known as *echelles*. The sleeves ended at the elbow in flounces of silk or lace. This garment may seem very formal to us today, but it was considered a state of undress when compared to the formality of Court attire. Louis XIV disapproved of the mantua, while the Duchesse d'Orleans complained, 'I don't know why people have so many styles of dress . . . I have never worn a *robe de chambre* nor a mantua . . . I find Court dress much more convenient than mantuas, which I can't endure.'

The mantua was, as Geoffrey Squire reminds us, the first outer garment to be made by women for women. 'From about 1675, as the making of female clothing began to pass from the province of the tailor to that of the dressmaker, femininity became for the first time a very conscious attribute of dress.' This is a significant point, indicating the emancipation of women's clothes from the autocracy of the Court tailors. In France, the Guild of Master Tailors reserved the right to make women's dresses, while the seamstresses, or *couturières*, made underclothes and negligees and, since it was a loose robe, the mantua. In England, mantua-making was entirely a trade for women—a 'genteel and profitable employ', wrote a social commentator, 'many of them living well and saving money'.

Also deriving from the *robe de chambre* was the prime dress worn by the ladies of eighteenth-century French society. This was the *sacque*, also called the *robe à la française*. In England, however, the popular dress for the most part of the eighteenth century remained the mantua. The *sacque* had, in place of a train, two wide pleats that fell from the back neckline to the floor, sometimes known as 'Watteau pleats'. The fabric of the petticoat and gown were sometimes shaped to accommodate the side hoops or paniers, their width as much as six feet across, the fabric richly embroidered with metallic thread. There is a mantua in the Victoria and Albert Museum that used 10 pounds of silver in the making.

Alternatives to the *sacque* were the loose, unwaisted tent-like *robe battante* and the billowing *robe volante*, that hung from the shoulders. These were said to have been invented, as the waspish Duchesse d'Orleans would have us believe, by Madame de Montespan, the King's mistress, who 'designed the *robe battante* to conceal her pregnancies, because this style of dress hid her figure. But when she appeared in them, it was precisely as if she had publicly announced that which she affected to conceal, for everybody at Court would say: "Madame de Montespan has put on her *robe battante* so she must be pregnant." '

In the 1790s new light muslin petticoats, with bouffant fichus around the neck and shoulders, were worn with the robe à l'anglaise. *Large hats and feathers balanced the bulk of the petticoat and overskirt. Sashes or belts, and fans were the essential accessories.*

In this portrait by Andrea Soldi of a musician in 1740, the sitter appears to be wearing a bag wig. His coat is lined with squirrel fur, a common feature of men's clothes and by this time no longer associated with wealth and privilege.

For much of the eighteenth century fashions were more or less static, but by the end of the century fashions would be fast paced, some enduring only a year, others merely for a season. Before the century was out, fashion would adopt the Liberty Cap of the Revolution, not to mention the rather grotesque fad of wearing miniature guillotine earrings . . .

Many people still found it deplorable that 'The rage for fashion and finery spreads from the highest to the lowest, and in

26

public places . . . it is very difficult to guess at rank in society or the heaviness of their purse.' In 1700 men might have one or two small, neat wigs and the women elaborate *coiffures*, but by 1772 the wig was *démodé* and there were 'at present three or four hundred methods of dressing the hair of a man of fashion'. Women were obliged to carry their effects in their petticoat pockets when Louis XIV was on the throne, but by mid century the handbag or 'indispensible' had been introduced.

The eighteenth century was an exciting age, an age in a hurry to shrug off the stultifing rule of the aristocracy, to embrace trade and expansion, and to enjoy the new wealth engendered by the middle class. It is a matter of dispute whether or not fashions reflect the spirit of the age. We cannot stop, we must go forward, and the wealth and conditions of our unique consumer society encourages this trend in our fashions. Were not men's clothes affected by the *zeitgeist*, by the spirit of commerce that characterized much of the eighteenth century? Men were now wearing the relatively new style of the three-piece suit: coat, waistcoat and breeches, with stockings and buckled shoes.

Men's clothes were to become progressively plainer except for Court costume. This, in the early eighteenth century, was also the three-piece suit but made of exceptionally fine silk, ornamented with gold thread, the waistcoat fringed at the hem, with large cuffs and a lace cravat.

Wigs were full-bottomed, long at both sides to the shoulders, and parted in the centre. They were made of human hair and for formal occasions powdered with wheat flour, a refinement introduced around 1700. Later a mixture of starch and plaster of Paris, sometimes tinted in a variety of colours, and strongly scented, was used. Plaiting the long curls of a wig, and tying it back with a bow, or wearing the back length confined in a black bag (originally a military style) known as a 'bag wig' was the gentleman's way of making life easier.

There were many variations on a theme. The Ramillies wig, for example, a long plait tied with two black bows, was named after one of Marlborough's victories over the French in 1706, when the officers are said to have tied their hair back in preparation for battle. Similarly, the cravat, which had its origins in seventeenth-century England, was worn in many styles, notably the popular Steinkirk which was tied with long ends hanging down, twisted together and held in place through a buttonhole of the wearer's coat.

Legend says that the fashion arose after the Battle of Steinkirk, when soldiers had no time to attend to their cravats before the action began, but there is no evidence to support this theory. The Steinkirk cravat appeared in the streets of London and Paris in 1692, and a month or two later in the American colonies, where European fashions were quickly noted.

'Negligence of loose attire' — The status of women

The emergent nation of pioneer settlers in America developed some of their own fashions in addition to those based on ideas from France and England. In view of the difference in the climate, especially in the south, modifications were essential. The banyan,

A Macaroni

—⟶—

Fashion has sporadic outbursts of eccentricity, such as the 'Incroyables' — the untidy, flamboyantly attired dandies of revolutionary France — and their precursors the Macaronis of London. Macaronis were young men of wealthy families who had made the customary tour of Italy and were inspired to emulate the Italian sense of style. They founded the Macaroni Club in 1764, and by the 1770s had gained some notoriety. They wore, on top of a monstrous toupet, a tiny Nivernois hat. Each sported a bouquet pinned to his lapel, and carried a tasseled cane which, they claimed, was an indispensible item, for without it a Macaroni could not raise his hat to a lady.

Riding habits for women in the eighteenth century copied the men's style of buttoning the coat left over right. In their long skirts women rode side-saddle, except those employed in the hazardous business of highway robbery, who wore breeches and sat astride. A merchant from Romford was so astonished at the appearance of a woman brandishing pistols that he fell off his horse, and was easily parted from his valuables.

originally a lightweight flannel jacket, had been adopted by British soldiers in India during the seventeenth century. An ideal loose gown, the banyan was worn by the fashionable in England and in France, made of soft silk for the summer and brocade or velvet for the winter. In America the banyan was termed a 'nightgown' although its primary use was not for wearing in bed, but as an informal garment for wearing about the house, with a linen shirt and breeches during the day.

During the long winters in Europe, both sexes wore wrapping robes, overcoats or cloaks. In France the heavy, flared and belted riding coat with its big protective collar and turned-back cuffs—the 'redingote'—was worn, as its name suggests, for riding and journeys by coach. Women wore a masculine-style waisted coat and long heavy skirt for riding. It was not especially popular with the men: 'I have been offended, let me tell you, my dear, at your new riding habit,' wrote Samuel Richardson to his niece in 1741, 'which is made so extravagantly in the mode that one cannot easily distinguish your sex by it. For you neither look like a modest girl in it, nor an agreeable boy.'

The roles played by men and women, in England anyway, were carefully defined. Women had to be the essence of femininity: modest, chaste, compliant—and silent. Men insisted on these virtues, and, for good measure, sometimes put it in writing: 'This modesty,' wrote John Gregory in 1750 to his daughters, 'which I think so essential in your sex, will naturally dispose you to be rather silent in company, especially in a large one.' This general attitude may account, in part, for the increasing femininity of women's fashions as the century progressed, and as men controlled the appearance of those women within the family circle. I find it difficult to believe that women did not, on the whole, ignore such gratuitous advice as that of the Reverent Wettenhall Wilkes to a 'Young Lady' in 1740: 'Never appear in company, without your stays. Make it your general rule, to lace in the morning, before you leave your chamber. The neglect of this, is liable to the censure of indolence, supineness of thought, sluttishness—and very often worse.

<blockquote>The negligence of loose attire
May oft' invite to loose desire.'</blockquote>

This contempt for and no doubt, fear of, women drew comment from the Abbé Le Blanc, who found in 1737 that 'The English lose a great deal in conversing so little with the sex whom nature has endowed with the graces; and whose company has constant charms, and a certain sweetness not to be found in men. Their presence and conversation polishes and softens men, and by the habit acquired of endeavouring to please them, a more agreeable tone of voice is contracted . . . But the English seem to fear the company of women, as much as the French delight in it.'

'A striking indication of wealth'— The commercialization of fashion

Obviously, the spirit of fashion is more likely to thrive creatively in an atmosphere where women are admired by men—and can take pride in themselves. Yet, as Neil McKendrick has shown, it was in England that the commercialization of fashion took place, in the

eighteenth century. 'The fashion doll, the fashion print, the fashion magazine, the fashion advertisement, the fashion shops, the great manufacturers making fashion goods and the hordes of those selling them were all agents in pursuit of new levels of consumption from an ever-widening market.'

London was, according to contemporary accounts, the brilliantly-lit shop window of Europe. In 1790 the Russian traveller Nikolai Karamzin was astonished. 'Never having seen anything like this I did not wonder at the error of a certain German prince who, upon entering London at night and seeing the streets brilliantly lighted, believed that the city had been illuminated for his arrival. The English people like light, and they give the government millions to replace the sun artificially. What a striking indication of a nation's wealth!'

There are many reasons for this upsurge of wealth, but maritime supremacy, colonial expansion, and, of course, the stirrings of the Industrial Revolution were major factors. There were also, as McKendrick points out, new techniques of marketing that exploited not only an existing demand, but also a potential demand, thereby creating a *new* market. The English had, to their advantage, a huge and aggressive textile industry, especially in wool. The need to produce more goods encouraged those historic inventions that played a major part in the Industrial Revolution, and gave fashion such a fresh impetus.

The first of these was Kay's flying shuttle, invented in 1733, which took weaving from the cottage parlour to the factory floor. In weaving the shuttle bearing the yarn has to be passed across the loom from hand to hand. Kay's invention speeded up the process since the weaver could perform single handed what had originally required two men. With the arrival of the shuttle came the need for a faster means of spinning to produce enough thread for the now hungry looms. The Lancashire inventor James Hargreaves submitted an idea—to the Royal Society of Arts—for a machine that drew out and twisted the wool or cotton, flax or hemp, six threads at a time, and would the yarn onto the bobbin.

The idea was later exploited by the dynamic, entrepreneurial (and notoriously rude) Richard Arkwright who devised a powered 'waterframe' spinning machine in 1769. The final phase in mechanized spinning was reached with Samuel Crompton's spinning 'mule' which produced cloth of a much finer quality than previously available, and was the equivalent of 'four million women with four million spinning wheels, only faster'.

In France silk weaving was improved in 1808 by Joseph-Marie Jacquard's punch card system of automatic pattern weaving, using a system not unlike the automatic piano roll, while, in America in 1793, a law graduate from Yale, Eli Whitney, invented a simple machine for extracting cotton from the seeds. Whitney's 'cotton gin' enabled an operator to extract and clean 50 lbs of cotton per day, compared to the one pound per day output from hand picking. The invention totally revolutionized productivity and affected even the social life of the southern states.

The fabric of high fashion was still silk—silk from Florence, from Lyon, and Spitalfields in London. By the end of the eighteenth century, cottons were much in demand—a demand

One of the simplest inventions in the history of textile manufacture was Eli Whitney's 'cotton gin', which stripped the raw fibre from the cotton seed, employing a spiked drum operated by a handle, much like the mechanism used in a musical box.

which had been created by the now powerful mills in the north of England—so that dresses were made of calicoes, muslin, lawn and cambric, while both cotton and linen were used for underwear. Men's clothes took advantage of the hard-wearing qualities of wool, worsted and broadcloth.

One could easily trace the progress of Conspicuous Consumption (a term coined by historian and economist Thorstein Veblen in 1899 to describe the 'consumption of goods which is ostentatious and intended to impress') through the history of lace. Subject to sumptuary laws, it had long been the prime adornment of the costumes of privilege. Until the nineteenth century, lace was always hand made, notably by the Huguenots in Buckingham-

'The Swing', or 'Les Hasards Heureux de l'Escarpolette', by Fragonard, one of the great, virtuoso painters of eighteenth-century France, who recorded the sensual, voluptuous aspects of the rococo. The lady's dress is certainly a robe à la française, *which she wears with a little bergère hat.*

shire, England, by the Flemish in Honiton, Devon; and in Europe at Valenciennes, Brussels, Torchon, Alençon and Venice, the centres of industry giving their name to the various types.

Fashions benefitted from the increased variety and quality of the cloth, but the styles of the dresses themselves, in the 'immutable cycles of fashion', took their natural course. In 1701 the rococo was launched. If an art movement and style can be said to have had an official send-off, the rococo did when Louis XIV, planning the design of the little Château de la Ménagerie for the teenage Duchesse de Bourgogne, told his architect that there must be a youthful note, an air of childhood everywhere. The rococo seemed the essence of movement, light, and informality, its flounced silks and satins replacing the ornate velvets and brocades of the baroque.

Perhaps the most sure eye to capture, for posterity, the spirit of the age and spirit of fashion was the painter Fragonard. His most famous painting 'The Swing', almost a cliché, is a wonderfully evocative image nonetheless, free of any restraint and full of charm, lightness, humour, sexual frivolity. There is a froth of light cottons and frills, ribbons and lace, of tumbling foliage, a flying slipper, and the courtly attention of men dressed in silk and velvet waistcoats, breeches, and with powdered wigs.

Fragonard's masterpiece was painted in the mid 1760s when the rococo was giving way to neoclassicism, yet the mantua, now a century old, was still going strong in England as the *robe à l'anglaise*. It was simpler than the *sacque*, but had a fitted bodice or stays, lightly boned, with a higher waistline and fewer flounces. Worn around the neck was a 'fichu' or neckerchief of lawn or muslin, frilled with lace. Straw hats were popular—a rustic touch —and both men and women affected the fashion of carrying large muffs in cold weather.

The fish from Les Halles— The influence of Pompadour

The rococo movement was in part guided by the delicate hand of Madame de Pompadour, patroness of the arts and of the painter Boucher in particular. The style is highly decorative and curvaceous, characterized by its cherubs or putti, its plasterwork (like the icing on a wedding cake) and the ornate ormolu gilding, a style that takes its name from the *rocaille* shellwork of grottoes and gardens. The rococo enhanced femininity and gave an impetus, then much needed, to eighteenth century fashions. Those art critics, the Goncourt brothers, described the rococo as being, 'that indefinable touch that bestows upon women a charm, a coquetry, a beauty that is beyond mere physical beauty . . . the smile of a contour, the soul of a form, the spiritual physiognomy of matter.'

No small wonder that Madame de Pompadour, elegant, charming, stylish, forceful, but no great beauty, encouraged such artists as Boucher and La Tour to the finer excesses of voluptuous painting, which the Goncourts described as 'elegant vulgarity'. A style of dress became *mode à la Pompadour*. She was honoured with a number of dishes, notably *filets de sole Pompadour*, a pun on her name which, before she became a Marquise, was plain Jeanne Poisson . . .

The Marquise de Pompadour, wearing an elaborate robe à la française, *painted by the Court painter Boucher, in 1759. Boucher's popularity was immense, not least with his patron, the Marquise. A contemporary account decided that, 'Boucher's brush is a magic agent inducing in us a state of tender admiration which suspends the functions of the mind.'*

Highrise Hairstyles

*Enormous and absurd head-
dresses were fashionable in the
mid eighteenth century, such as
this topical representation of the
Battle of Bunker's Hill in the
War of Independence. The
engraving is a cartoon, but was
probably not all that
exaggerated. The elaborate
constructions were often made
with the subject's own hair,
with additional false pieces,
held in place by paste and
pomatum, and stuffed with
horsehair. Once completed they
were preserved for several
weeks, since a great deal of time
and effort, not to mention
expense, had gone into their
making.
Ladies had to sleep sitting
upright, their head-dresses
enclosed in a protective bag.
This provided a temptation to
the mice that infested most
houses, and the pregnant Lady
Coke of Norfolk reputedly
miscarried on finding an
uninvited guest in her coiffure.
One lady, as reported in the*
London Magazine *of 1768, had
her head-dress 'opened' after
nine weeks (sic). In defence of
her style she remarked that 'If
one did not dress like other
people, one should be pointed
out as one went along.'*

Boucher's portrait of her, posing in a garden, is one of the most seductive portraits of the eighteenth century, decidedly idealized and yet capturing her warm, forthright personality and enchanting dress. It is a *robe à la française*. She wears her hair characteristically short and combed back—one of the styles the Court were 'driven mad' to imitate. A lace ruff is around her neck, a rose pinned to the left of her *décolletage*. The sleeves and the *engageantes* (the frills) of ruffled lace at the elbows, and bows match the *échelles* on her stomacher. The silk gown and petticoat are probably worn over a buckram petticoat, itself worn over a hoop. There is the glimpse of a tiny, buckled shoe.

The Court thought her an adventuress, a parvenu, the incarnation of the Paris bourgeoisie, a fish from Les Halles. She may have been all of these things, save the latter, but she had an instinct for fashion and a way with kings. Nancy Mitford describes her presentation to Louis XV, whose mistress she became, accompanied by the Comtesse de Lachau-Montaubon and the Comtesse d'Estrades.

'They all wore thickly embroidered satin skirts over enormous paniers; short muslin sleeves; small white feathers, held in place over their lightly-powdered hair with diamonds; and narrow trains.' The Marquise faced the King and 'her three curtseys were impeccable, and masterly was the kick with which she got her train out of the way so that she could walk backwards, the most difficult part of the whole proceeding.'

'No more extravaganzas'— The end of the eighteenth century

Towards the end of the century the back-fullness profile of women's clothes was reaching its apex, the protuberance being echoed by the fullness of the bosom—often artificially created by cork padding or gauze. The robe was drawn up in three flounces or drapes to give a gathered bustle, bordered with silk flounces or decorated with bows, worn over a petticoat with a simple ruffled border. This was the *robe à la polonaise*.

Some suggest that this style probably developed from the habit women had when walking, of stuffing the burden of super-fluous material into slashes or pockets at the side of the petticoat, designed for that purpose. But the *polonaise* is really a stylized development of the mantua. The draped skirt, worn over a simple quilted petticoat, is anchored in much the same way as the mantua, at two points over the rump.

This was the direction in which the profile was heading, towards a more pronounced back-fullness, and the *polonaise* was the means of achieving this, just as the mantua had been over a century before. Whether the reasons were practical or inevitable and predestined according to the mysterious laws of cause and effect is debatable. Over the following decades the back-fullness was attained by a bustle worn with a short-tail bolero-like jacket known as a 'spencer'. By 1790–93 the waistline had crept higher to anticipate the imminent arrival of the neoclassic, tubular cycle, which had been waiting in the wings.

The eighteenth century began with an inflexible mon-archy, and ended with its demise. Marie Antoinette, encouraged

'Le Rendez-vous pour Marly', *1776, by the engraver and illustrator Moreau le Jeune. Moreau made charming and intimate studies of social life, and he carefully observed dress details. The ladies are wearing the* polonaise *dress, which first appeared in France in 1772. The fashion was not Polish, but it coincided with the partition of Poland. A development of the mantua, the design may have come from the* robe relevée dans les poches, *where the ample material was lifted up and gathered into slits or pockets provided at the sides of the petticoat.*

by close women friends at Court, spent lavishly and extravagantly. She maintained, for a brief spell, the dazzling splendour of the costumes of power, but it all ended in a cart ride down the Rue St Honoré, the source of Paris fashions, to the guillotine in the Place Louis XV. As fashion went though, she showed the world how it should be done. Unfortunately, she didn't know how to stop.

'In 1786 the Queen's bills from Mademoiselle Bertin were so astronomical as to give sleepless nights to her mistress of the robes ... Even the Queen took fright on hearing that she had spent 87,594 livres in a single year, which did not include the bills of the Court dressmaker Madame Eloffe, nor the 31,000 francs spent on the riding habits from her English tailor.'

Her passion for fashion was to help bring about her fate. She may have had a faint presentiment of it when she remarked to Mademoiselle Bertin, the milliner and dress designer who had done much to encourage her excesses: 'No more flowers and feathers, no more extravaganzas.'

Chapter 3

THE AGE OF TON
1790–1840

From about 1800 to 1830 the English Regency period had its French counterpart in the Empire or *Directoire* style. Women's clothes were simple, high-waisted white muslin dresses, worn with nothing much underneath. As feminine fashions headed towards a romantic 'Quality Street' era of bonnet, ringlet curls and demure shyness—all petticoats, lace and flounces—so men had their final sartorial fling in the age of the dandy before Victorian conformity took over. Every period has its leaders of mens' fashion, but the Regency was unique in producing two archetypal dandies who became legendary—Beau Brummel and Count d'Orsay. The French Ambassador to London, Chateaubriand, noted with alarm that English Society spent much of its time dressing. Dressing for lunch, dressing for a stroll down Bond Street or through Hyde Park. They dressed to dine at half-past seven, dressed again for the opera, and again at midnight for an evening party. 'The supreme height of fashion,' the Ambassador said, 'was to be unable to make one's way into the small rooms of a private ball, to remain on the staircase blocked by the crowd.'

A portrait was exhibited in 1783 at the Salon du Louvres, in Paris, that provoked a storm of protest. The subject was Marie Antoinette, simply attired in a white muslin dress, a large straw hat adorned with plumes, and holding a rose in her left hand. The picture conveys the essence of femininity and charm, the more so since the artist was a woman—Elizabeth Vigée Lebrun—whom Joshua Reynolds pronounced to be 'finer than Vandyke'.

Public indignation at the portrait seems to have been confined to the Queen's dress which, said her critics, made her look like a chambermaid. In fact, Marie Antoinette was only expressing the ideal of the rustic life which inspired her famous dairy or *hameau* at Trianon, but which nonetheless had been an expensive enterprise: 'A lot of money has been spent on giving the Queen's *hameau* the aspect of poverty,' wrote the Marquis de Bombelles, 'but by spending a little more, Her Majesty would have been able to improve the conditions of those who are really poor.'

If the portrait was interpreted as an image of a decadent monarchy mocking a nation on the verge of bankruptcy, it served to emphasize the Queen's unpopularity—the dress itself was of little consequence. This may be confirmed by the fact that three similar portraits had passed without comment: Vigée Lebrun's delightful self-portrait, and her portraits of the Duchesse de Polignac and the Comtesse Du Barry, wearing the white muslin garment variously known as the *chemise de la reine*, the *robe en gaulle*, and the *robe à la mode de créole*. Of this attire the artist

Never before, and certainly not since antiquity, had so little been worn by so many women, nor had fashionable ladies been so charmingly décolleté. *Hairstyles were short, and worn with false braids and topknots. From the* Lady's Magazine *for 1811.*

Vigée Lebrun's portrait of Marie Antoinette in a muslin chemise dress, or robe en gaulle, *or* robe à la mode de créole. The style originated in the French West Indies, and a fashion note was the grenadine flower worn in one's hat, said to celebrate the (short-lived) recapture of Grenada by the French, from the British, in 1779. Historical events were often the source of fashionable accessories, although they did not affect the basic shape of dresses.

herself said, 'I wore only white gowns of muslin or lawn . . . My hair cost me nothing, I styled it myself. As I despised the costume then worn by women, I tried in every way to make it picturesque and was delighted when I obtained the confidence of my sitters who allowed me to drape them as I pleased.'

Fashion goes Greek

If one accepts the claims made by art historian Joseph Baillio, Vigée Lebrun was largely responsible for launching the style that came to be known as the 'Empire' line. 'Perhaps more than any single individual in the last quarter of the eighteenth century, Vigée Lebrun influenced the development of women's costume. She helped to popularize a more natural look by introducing into her portraiture light-weight gowns, as opposed to the corseted and bulky *robes à la française* which had long been in vogue. She also spurned the great masses of ornately dressed and powdered wigs women were forced to endure to be fashionable in favour of natural hair.

The *robe en gaulle* had been introduced into France and America by the Creoles of Martinique in the French West Indies. It appeared in Paris, and later in Philadelphia. The dress was tied by cords under the bust and at the waist, and worn with a high-placed sash, and a ribbon securing the frilly neckline. The robe might be worn with a lightly-boned bodice or stays, or simply with

The mode à la grecque *reached America, influencing not only the fashions but interior design and furniture as well. The dress here, worn with the Titus-cut hair style, was photographed in the American Museum in Bath, England, in a reproduction of a neoclassic interior.*

The high waist, the floppy rustic hat and white muslin dress are features of the style so beautifully recorded in Gainsborough's romantic, ethereal portraits, which may have inspired this picture of Lady Elizabeth Foster by the Swiss artist Angelica Kauffmann, in 1786.

a stout cotton lining. Below the waist the dress was full, being gathered at the front, and pleated over the back and padded rump.

By 1789 the *Lady's Magazine* was able to comment, 'All the sex now—from fifteen to fifty upwards (I should rather say downwards) appear in their white muslin frocks, with broad sashes, with their hair curled over their foreheads, and hanging down behind, to the bottom of their backs—and all without caps.' During the space of five years the muslin chemise had become the style *à la grecque*, where the front hung straight down from the high waistline, while retaining a trace of the back-fullness profile.

The high-waisted chemise dress, was called the 'Empire' line because the style coincided more or less with the establishment of Napoleon as Emperor of France. The dress is supposed to have symbolized the new republic acknowledging the ancient republic of Greece, inspired by the Ionic chiton once worn by Greek women. The *chemise à la grecque* first appeared about 1795, and was made of fine, almost transparent muslin, and hung straight down from the waist to the floor, and with a considerable train.

---

*T*he chemise being inspired by classical antiquity was worn for a while with sandals, and one's natural hair was cut short, or braided *à l'antique*, or with a short wig *à la grecque* worn with a headband. The style coincided in France with a sort of '*apres-revolution*' wear—a passing fascination with the macabre, and a celebration that the Terror was finally over. Apart from the fad for guillotine earrings already mentioned, the fashionable citizen sported a *ceinture à la victime*, a blood-red ribbon that had been placed around the neck of those on their way to execution. Hairstyles cropped *à la victime* or *sacrifié* were briefly popular. There was even a '*Bal de Victime*' in Paris. Invitations were extended only to those who had lost relatives to the falling blade during the Revolution.

In England a tax on hair powder in 1795 hurried the demise of the wig, and encouraged natural hair. For women, hairdressers recommended the 'Titus' cut, where hair was 'cut close to the roots so as to restore its natural stiffness and make it grow in a perpendicular direction'. The fashionable ideal, though, was the short, bouncy curls and simple headband as pictured in David's portrait of the famous beauty Jeanne Récamier in her Empire dress, reclining on an Empire sofa. Together with Germaine de Staël she was the nucleus of Paris salons for over fifty years. In London, Jeanne Récamier was followed by a throng of admiring onlookers through Kensington Gardens.

The Greek style revealed the natural curves of the body—and some unwelcome ones, since the general principle was to discard corsets and stays; at the most one might wear lightly-boned taffeta corsets. Women less shapely than Jeanne Récamier resorted to a type of long corset to maintain the ideal shape.

Given the flimsiness of the garment, shawls came into their own, and some women did wear a chemise or simple petticoat, and some a skin-tight undergarment. Even so, women shivered, especially in inclement Albion, where in one year 'eighteen ladies caught fire and eighteen thousand caught cold'. A

Free, Amazonian ladies with their flowing cashmere shawls and Empire-line dresses celebrated the arrival of the new century. 'The pretty girls and goddesses sweep the muddy streets of the capital with the trains of their long, transparent dresses,' observed the French writer Louis Sebastien Mercier, who patently approved of the style.

chronicler of the 1790s, Louis Sebastien Mercier, was moved to write, 'I don't know whether these dancers were great admirers of Republican Greece but at any rate they had modelled their attire on that of Aspasia; naked arms, bared bosoms, sandals on their feet, hair twisted and plaited around their heads—the fashionable hairdressers take their styles from the antique busts . . . For some time the chemise has been banished, it only disfigures the natural forms and moreover was a useless article of apparel. The corset of flesh-coloured silk tricot which clings to the body does not hide but rather discloses secret charms.'

Men, not unnaturally, were much taken by the style, at least in France. In America the *fin-de-siècle* Paris dresses caused a sensation, especially the dress worn by Elizabeth Patterson of Baltimore when 'mobs of boys crowded around her splendid equipage to see what I hope will not often be seen in this country, an almost naked woman . . . her appearance was such that it threw all the company into confusion and no one dared look at her but by stealth . . . Her dress was the thinnest silk and white crêpe without the least stiffening in it, made without a single pleat in the skirt, the width at the bottom being made of gores; there was scarcely any waist and her arms were uncovered and the rest of her form visible.'

Classic versus romantic

The change in style from the *sacque* and the *polonaise* to the *robe à la grecque* may appear rather abrupt, but in fact was transitional and took about fifteen to twenty years, through the *robe en gaulle*, the back-fullness chemise, to the Empire line. The transitions are so gradual, as Agnes Young points out, that people are seldom aware that a change is taking place. 'When one of the dominant cycle types is drawing towards its close, and is about to make way for its successor, it begins slowly to lose its characteristic appearance and to assume some of the features of the type which is soon to succeed it.'

Did the art movement known as the neoclassic or Greek revival determine this change, from the back-fullness to the 'tubular' cycle which followed, thus supporting the *zeitgeist* theory that fashions are influenced by the 'spirit of the age'? Or was it mere coincidence that the tubular style, inevitably due to appear at the turn of the century according to Young's 35-year cycles of change (the back-fullness began in 1760 and ended in 1795), admirably suited the *mode à la grecque*? Young's 'Theory of Inevitability' suggests that even if there had not been a hellenistic style, the tubular cycle would have occurred anyway, its perpendicular character enhancing a different fashion.

The source of the *mode à la grecque* was the neoclassical style which deposed the rococo movement about 1760. Painting, architecture, sculpture, furniture and fashions all fell under the spell of the craze for the antique, all susceptible to the 'indefinable breath of the spirit of the age', as Victoria Sackville-West put it in 1944. She was, in fact, referring to the whimsical and coexistent English Gothic revival, as featured in James Wyatt's Fonthill Abbey, and Horace Walpole's Strawberry Hill—all towers and battlements and stucco. At least their style was English.

There had been in Britain, throughout the eighteenth century, especially during the rough-and-tumble age of Hogarth, a resistance to French culture. The exceptions were the fashionable who found it necessary to envelop themselves in huge black bags when venturing into the street—a precaution probably unique in fashion history—for fear of being jeered at, then a popular English pastime. 'As the world of honest enjoyment became more and more defiantly English, the world of fashion became more and more French,' wrote Derek Jarrett surveying Hogarth's London. But French fashions as always prevailed, and the intellectual element of neoclassicism was far more powerful than any efforts of the bucolic English to resist.

The neoclassic style took its inspiration in part from the excavations in the mid eighteenth century of the ancient sites at Herculaneum and Pompeii, and the adjacent temples of Paestum. Impetus to the movement was also given by the archeologist Johann Winckelmann, and by such travellers as Stuart and Revitt who published their book *Antiquities of Athens* in 1762, and by the fanciful poetry of Ossian (or James Macpherson), who was called the 'Homer of the North'.

Romanticism was already undermining the purity of the classic ideal. A pity really, for there was never a fashion more suited to the Greek concept of *eos*—the dawn of a new century—than the clean, unfussy, supple and flowing robes of the *robe à la grecque*. Perhaps the fashion was too simple, too restrictive, and wanting of the embellishments and decorative potential of a style with a future. In short, there was no room for improvement, and no opportunity for versatility, unless the style adopted—dare one say it—a more romantic appeal or a mere caprice. 'Paris—The women's dress is affectedly simple—white muslin, very short waists, very full petticoats: but the ugliest part of their habiliments is the high chimneys on their hats, which chimneys are covered with feathers and flowers. When fashion is subject to taste, I like it, but when it is despotic and capricious, and subverts all taste, I cannot endure it. To my idea, the more nearly women's dress assimilates to the antique, the more beautiful.' Thus spake Lady Barbara Charlton of the fashions of 1814.

They had not changed much over the past decade. The high waist prevailed; it was such a dominant, fundamental while not entirely unprecedented feature, that only the arrival of the fuller skirt and the bell-shaped cycle could bring it down. The most notable aspect was the emphasis on the bosom, elevated by the high waistline, and revealed by the low-cut *décolletage*. Sleeves now covered the arms to the wrists and big bonnets were definitely the thing, as Jane Austen wrote in one of her bulletins to her sister: 'I am amused by the present style of female dress; the coloured petticoats with braces over the white spencers and enormous Bonnets on the full stretch, are quite entertaining. It seems to me a more marked change than one has seen—Long sleeves appear universal, even in *Dress*, the waist short, and as far as I have been able to judge, the Bosom covered—Petticoats short, and generally, tho' not always, flounced.'

In England, and while Jane Austen was noting with her keen eye the modes and manners of her age, the period known as

An opera dress featured in the magazine La Belle Assemblée *in 1816, and designed by London's most fashionable dressmaker, Mrs Bell of Bloomsbury. Her reputation was not harmed by the fact that she was the wife of the magazine's publisher.*

the Regency was well under way. The Regency absorbed the Empire style, pondered for a brief while, and then recycled it for home consumption, but cautiously. 'I have no reason to suppose long sleeves are allowable,' said Jane. 'I have lowered the bosom, especially at the corners, and plaited black satin ribbon around the top . . . Mrs Tilson had long sleeves too, and she assured me that they are worn in the evening by many. I was glad to hear this.'

Jane Austen, in common with her contemporaries and irrespective of their worldliness, was in thrall to the tyranny of fashion; Paris might be the arbiter of taste, but what really mattered was what everyone else was doing. In turn-of-the-century Paris, and in London, the fashionable wore their natural hair short, with perhaps a matching hairpiece, with a variety of ornaments—jewels, feathers, braids, chignons and combs.

French day dresses and morning suits of 1822. This was the year when waistlines first began to descend to normal level, and both men and women wore corsets to accentuate narrow waists. In this fashion plate, the man is clean shaven and with the Byronic curls of the romantic period. He wears a stock or neckcloth, and has M-cut notches in his morning coat revers, or lapels.

The lady wears a pelisse robe, later called a redingote, a French word derived from the English 'riding coat' which buttoned down the front to the hem. He wears pantaloons fastened under the instep, a Wellington hat, and carries a cane, de rigueur *for all fashionable gentlemen.*

But what were they doing in Boston, Massachusetts? 'Now Mamma, what do you think I am going to ask for? — a wig. Eleanor has got a new one just like my hair and only five dollars . . . At the Assembly I was quite ashamed of my head, for nobody has long hair.' If one was ever in doubts as to what should be worn, the fashion magazines of the day (they began to appear, in Paris, at the end of the eighteenth century) could be reassuring in helping one appease what has variously been called the 'invincible tyrant', the 'Great Mogul' and 'the despotic Goddess' of fashion.

'A lemon-coloured sarsnet dress,' advised *La Belle Assemblée* firmly, 'trimmed with an embroidery of roses: a white lace drapery with train, fastened down the front with topaz snaps; a richly embroidered scarf is thrown carelessly across the shoulders. Topaz necklace and earrings. The hair in loose ringlet curls,

*A dinner dress of 1824.
Skirts had begun to fill out in 1816
with gores inserted to give width, and
decorative features such as bows,
flounces, ribbons and floral designs to
emphasize the expanding hem. The
puffed sleeves at the shoulder
gradually filled out to compliment the
skirt, reaching the exaggerated gigot
sleeves of the 1830s.*

divided by an ornamental comb. Gloves and shoes of white or lemon-coloured kid. A bouquet of natural flowers.'

They might have added a parasol, especially one in plaid. They were by now very fashionable, but had been ridiculed towards the end of the previous century. A man sporting an umbrella was taking a risk, but not, however, if the man was George Bryan Brummell. Brummell was not intimidated by the 'Great Mogul'—he *was* the Great Mogul! In her book *The Dandy*, Ellen Moers wrote of that fashionable Regency man: 'To specify his role among his contemporaries requires the words *fashion*, *ton*, *exclusive*, and *the world* used in the exact sense and with all the intimacy that the Regency gave them. Brummell had only to look upon or speak to a man to make him fashionable, and only to cut another to make him a pariah.'

The age of the dandy

The early nineteenth century was the age of the dandy, and it is reasonable to ask why, following the age of bloody revolutions, there arose in England the phenomenon of foppery. In a letter written in 1778, John Wilkes, resplendently attired in a blue suit and silk waistcoat edged with gold and fastened with pearl buttons, assured his daughter Polly that he was 'undoubtedly the greatest fop in Bath'. Moers suggests that 'Dandyism was a product of the revolutionary upheavals of the late eighteenth century. When such solid values as wealth and birth are upset, ephemera such as style and pose are called upon to justify the stratification of society.'

Dandyism, as exemplified by Brummell, used fashion as a weapon in the class war which the English are so constantly preoccupied with and committed to. The dandy, by his close attention to personal cleanliness—Brummell was said to have spent at least two hours every morning washing and scrubbing himself before putting on his immaculate attire—condemned the legions of 'great unwashed'. Equally, the dandy condemned the aristocracy and monarchy yet, in one respect, resembled the nobility in its indolence, viewing the march of progress with indifference, relishing his 'superiority, irresponsibility, inactivity'.

The Beau dressed not flamboyantly but with studied reserve and understatement—again, an English characteristic. Brummell's puritanical obsession with his appearance may be due in part to the fact that he was a small man physically, and in part to the fact that he had risen from the servant class, who often knew more about how a gentleman should behave than the gentlemen themselves. He was perhaps compensating for his inferiority, and what he sought in fashion was security through power—power through the medium of manners and exquisite taste. Brummell made fashion important by setting standards that could hardly be equalled, although many tried. Said the French author Stendhal, 'For them, fashion is not a pleasure, it's a duty.'

English tailoring was widely acknowledged to be the finest in the world, the French in particular being impressed by the seemingly casual 'country style' affected by Englishmen of fashion. This style arose from the 'squirearchy', as it has been termed. There was no counterpart in France to the hunting fraternity of the

eighteenth and nineteenth centuries in England—wealthy, eccentric, solidly conservative and firmly rooted in an immutable class structure. Riding clothes were adopted for daytime dress, perhaps out of expedience since following the hounds was for many a full-time occupation.

Styles in the frock or dress coat were also born of expedience. The front of the coat was cut away across the waist leaving the tails to fall behind, allowing the wearer greater freedom on

Beau Brummell was a discriminating, conservative perfectionist. 'One of his general maxims', reported a fellow dandy, 'was that the severest mortification which a gentleman could incur, was to attract observation in the street by his outward appearance.'

47

An American gentleman at the turn of the century. The 'Puritan' hat with the narrowing crown was about to be supplanted by the beaver, or top hat, but the overcoat and cape, similar to the Ulster, were worn throughout the first half of the nineteenth century.

horseback. The tail coat became fashionable in London and Paris for daytime wear. It eventually became, of course, the ultimate in elegant, formal attire as worn by Fred Astaire, in *Top Hat*.

The active, daily routine of the country squire, like that of his military counterpart the 'officer and gentleman', needed a high standard of tailoring to produce a robust garment that must also appear elegant, understated and discreet, the style that Brummell endorsed and carried to the limits. The tailors themselves became the arbiters of taste in menswear, and their official publication, *The Tailor & Cutter*, was and is the authoritative voice of the profession.

The Dandy Duke

The Regency was the age of *haut ton*, or style. Ton is manners, morals, deportment and dress. Ton was the exclusive property of the world of rank and fashion but not necessarily of culture and learning. The Regency, with its eye on the neoclassical ideals of order, logic and restraint, riding insecurely on the back of hedonism, produced the dandy as the symbol of the age. There were many candidates for the appellation 'dandy' and in the first decade of the nineteenth century Brummell was the leader of the pack, yet stood apart from it since others could not quite measure up to his demands of perfection. A hard man, was the Beau, as hard on himself as on others.

His dress coat was blue—a tasteful blue, of course, with simple brass buttons, and tightly buttoned across in the cut-away style, with the tails ending just above and behind the knee. The lapels rose to a collar that enclosed a lightly starched and perfectly tied cravat. The Beau's cravats were perhaps the most famous feature of his attire. 'These', said his valet, in a legendary story, displaying an armful of linen cravats, 'were this morning's failures.' Under the coat an inch or two of buff-coloured waistcoat was to be seen, and two links—only two—of a gold watchchain. Buckskin pantaloons also in buff and of course perfectly fitting, went just below the knee where they tucked into Hessian boots. It was said he cleaned his boots with the froth of champagne. Brummell's evening wear was marginally more modest than that of the daytime—a blue woollen coat, linen cravat, white waistcoat, black pantaloons buttoned at the ankles, silk stockings and neat pumps with oval toes. Clean shaven and precisely *coiffured*, off he went to White's club.

Brummell's style inspired a generation of men, who took to wearing dark, woollen suits with a waistcoat, and pantaloons or breeches. The Duke of Wellington was respectably dandified and had even been nicknamed 'The Dandy' and it was arguable which of the two adversaries on the field of battle was the more elegant—the Duke or Napoleon Bonaparte. Like Brummell, Napoleon was a perfectionist in all things and small in stature, although the extraordinary portrait by David of him in all his regal splendour like a sartorial Zeus makes him appear larger than life.

In matters of dress, the Emperor gave two things to posterity—the black, cocked bicorne hat and the hairstyle, with the locks brushed forward over his forehead—oh, and the habit of sticking his hand in a vent in his waistcoat, said to be due to

chronic indigestion. In company with the fastidious Beau, Napoleon had a tail coat, waistcoat and tight breeches tucked into his boots, and was also clean shaven. But while Bonaparte's preoccupation with his appearance was due to an overweening vanity, Brummell's may have been due to deeper motives of the psyche.

Having slid further and further into debt due, it is said, to gambling losses, Brummell found refuge in exile in France, where he died in 1840, penniless, incontinent and raving. It is possible that the Beau's scrubbed cleanliness and his impeccable attire were the signs of an obsessional neurosis of which too-frequent washing is a common symptom. His behaviour may have been the only thing that maintained his sanity. In severely reduced circumstances and unable to maintain his obsession, he was finally tipped over the edge into delirium and death.

European styles were carefully noted and followed by the new Society in post-revolutionary America, but the cult of the dandy failed to take root in colonial circles. The man of fashion wore a frock coat, waistcoat and trousers, but many, especially the Quakers, still retained the eighteenth century knee-breeches until well into the first half of the nineteenth century.

Count d'Orsay. The dandy, through his singular obsession with his personal attire, carried the art of dress to exaggerated lengths and into the realm of narcissism. His cravats were whiter than white, his snuff boxes and jewellery spared no expense, his tailor fulfilling the role of counsellor, cutter, confidant and critic.

Count d'Orsay — 'As gay as a hummingbird'

Michael Sadleir, in *Blessington D'Orsay*, said that the dandies were 'a new band of aristocracy, and one all the more difficult to destroy because it will be based on qualities and gifts which toil cannot acquire nor money buy'. This new aristocracy took the place of the established but now fallen monarchy at the time of transition. The dandy was an arch snob, and his cold contempt was something that Gallic temperament could neither comprehend or emulate. Yet the most famous 'other dandy' of the times was a Frenchman — Gillion Gaspard Alfred de Grimaud, Comte d'Orsay et du Saint Empire — known in England where he lived for many years as Count d'Orsay.

While Brummell practised an almost monk-like asceticism, d'Orsay enjoyed the embellishments of the high priest; fashion was the religion common to both, and both men were literally celibate. Ellen Moers describes d'Orsay 'shimmering in pastel colours, soft velvets and silks, perfumes, jewels—all the fantasies of costume that Brummell disdained were part of d'Orsay's style. And while Brummell's costume had won a unanimous, quiet approval by its perfection, d'Orsay's inspired extended comment from the hostile and admiring alike.'

Count d'Orsay stood six feet three, with a magnificent physique, was splendidly handsome, impeccably groomed, gregarious and charming. He was, not to put too fine a point on it, too good to be true. If we apply the *zeitgeist* theory to Brummell and d'Orsay, the former reflected the spirit of neoclassicism, while the latter represented the Byronic romanticism. The painter Haydon saw him in a 'white great-coat, blue satin cravat, hair oiled and curling, hat of the primest curve and purest water, gloves scented with eau de Cologne or eau de jasmin, primrose in tint, skin in tightness.'

Thomas Carlyle of *Sartor Resartus* described the Count as being 'built like a tower, with floods of dark auburn hair, with a beauty, with an adornment unsurpassable on this planet.' Mrs Jane Carlyle, who remembered d'Orsay 'as gay in his colours as a humming bird' met him five years later when, in keeping with the more sombre fashions of the mid nineteenth century, he was dressed in black and brown—'a black satin cravat, a brown velvet waistcoat, a brown coat, some shades darker than the waistcoat, lined with velvet of its own shade and almost black trousers, one breast pin, a large pear-shaped pearl set into a little cup of diamonds, and only one fold of gold chain around his neck, tucked together right on the centre of his spacious breast with one magnificent turquoise.'

Certainly, Jane Carlyle didn't miss much but then she, like everyone else, was fascinated by the detail and was naturally very familiar with her husband's 'Philosophy of Clothes', as *Sartor Resartus* is subtitled. Dandyism, as is said of some wines, was a poor traveller, and needed to be experienced in the *pays d'origine* to savour its full bouquet. Until Oscar Wilde went to America, dandyism never ventured westwards, but was much appreciated by the American visitors to England. 'He is the divinity of dandies,' said an American fan of d'Orsay's, 'in another age he would have passed into the court of the gods, and youths would have sacrificed to the God of fashion!'

The key to the rigid discipline of true dandyism is sexuality, or rather, an apparent indifference to sex. There was no part in Brummell's life for matters sexual and it is said that his appeal to women was precisely that he was so 'unconquerable'. As for Count d'Orsay, 'He was so feebly sexed,' suggests Michael Sadleir, 'as to be virtually impotent—physically capable, maybe, of intercourse but without desire for it . . . Combined with his peculiar type of physical beauty—the build and stature of an athlete, the face of a woman—it explains his popularity with men, his lack of appeal to women.' Sexual desire undermines will and resolve and renders us all too human, while men like Brummell were super-

Embroidery, applied trimmings of frills, ribbons, flounces and piping and elaborate decorations of artificial flowers and leaves were a feature of early 1820s fashions. Even morning dresses, such as this one from Ackerman's Repository of Arts, *1824, ostensibly for modest at-home wear, were not spared the craze for over-decoration. Fabric was plentiful and, more importantly, labour was cheap.*

51

human. Whether their dandyism could be seen as psychotic behaviour, engendered by severely repressed sexual desires, is speculation best left to the Freudians.

Freedom of the soul

At a period when social values and stratas were in upheaval the dandy, by sheer virtue of fashion and ton, set formative standards at a high level of perfection. Dress, if all else was uncertain, would be the model for social security. For Beau Brummell the philosophy paid the additional dividend of self-aggrandizement: he set the rules and dandyism had perforce to live up to him, and not he to the concept of the dandy. Brummell both practised and preached the great tenet of fashion exclusiveness, and became the tyrant of manners in a bid to instruct and inspire an unstable hierarchy. He, of the servant class, was now obliged to show his masters how to behave before it became too late and the English monarchy followed the French monarchy into oblivion.

The age of the dandy can be said to have lasted for over fifty years, from Beau Brummell's appearance in Regency Society just prior to the beginning of the nineteenth century, to d'Orsay's death in Paris in 1852. The ways of their passing were appropriate to their ideals—Brummell's death was tragic, d'Orsay's romantic; the Count died while one of his nieces played a waltz tune on the piano. 'Play it faster,' d'Orsay urged, 'faster!'

Romanticism

Romanticism expresses the freedom of the soul and the spirit, as summed up by Victor Hugo: 'Freedom in literature, freedom in art, freedom in society.' The romantic is in tune with the spirit of nature, delighting in the violence, the turbulence, the disorder and destruction of nature. Where the face of classicism is serene, that of the romantic is troubled with a stormy brow. The fashionable romantic, claimed Chateaubriand, 'had to appear ill at first glance . . . he must have something neglected about his person, neither clean shaven nor fully bearded, but as if his beard had grown without warning in a moment of despair.' It was, however, an affordable despair, not the desperation of true poverty where fashion was unknown. It is strange that romanticism, which celebrates a breaking away from feudalism and the long-established social order, should look back to the Middle Ages for inspiration from chivalry.

The romantic treads a very fine line between sensitivity and sentimentality. In the 1820s there was a certain androgynous aspect to men's clothes—narrow, corseted waists to match those of women's costumes, leg-of-mutton sleeves, short hair and side whiskers like the short hair and side curls worn by women. But paradoxically men were supposed to be heroes—the ultimate of masculinity—and so women had to appear the ultimate of femininity (or have it thrust upon them) to be worthy of masculine chivalry—Lancelot and Guinevere, Tristan and Isolde.

Obligingly, and over two decades, women's fashions became a riot of flounces and laces and ribbons and bows, fragility, frivolity, bonnets and hemlines of unprecedented height. Femininity was emphasized by the purely non-functional char-

A ball dress from La Belle Assemblée, *1825. False curls and artificial flowers to match those flowers on the bodice and skirt were the height of* bon ton, *and a shawl was an essential accessory if only to keep the shoulders warm, since all evening wear was* décolleté. *The waistline had begun its gradual descent from 1823, and would not rise again until Paul Poiret re-introduced the style around 1910.*

acter of the costume—a prize to be taken, and gift-wrapped into the bargain, while men's clothes were becoming utilitarian. In an age when fashion was confirming its importance, the fact that men's clothes borrowed some elements of women's fashions merely acknowledged the powerful influence a style exerted over the fashionable world—the adrogyne was simply paying lip service to the 'goddess of fashion'.

Hairstyles, hats and accessories

Throughout the romantic era the Grecian style of hair persisted although it was increasingly ornate. In anticipation of the coming bell-shaped cycle, the straight-down, high-waisted Empire style began to fill out at the hem. In 1815 skirts were gored to form a slender cone, sleeves also filled out at the shoulder making a short puff. 'Never were short sleeves so much in favour,' wrote a Paris commentator in 1819, 'never before in Paris were pulmonary and nervous complaints so frequent. I sincerely hope, however, that next winter will bring along with its rigour, that modesty which can alone render a female desirable; and that as soon as ices and melons cease to be eaten, short sleeves will cease to be worn.'

Over the dress one might wear a spencer—a short jacket with a high collar and long sleeves—and, on the head, a poke bonnet abundantly floral. 'A curious romantic is adopted by some young ladies, in the ornamenting of their hats; it is aiming at the sentimental, but I call it acrostical. Suppose, for instance, a lady wearing the hat is named Maria: she accordingly sports a marsh-mallow blossom, an anemone, a rose, an iris and an asphodel or evening lily. This forms a mixture of colours and even of flowers, not always in season.' In the 1820s hats grew ever larger and were embellished by waves of plumes. Parsols, shawls and muffs completed the effect. Not quite—one had to have a bracelet. As Lady Harriet Granville wrote in a letter of 1824, 'You are not perhaps aware that a magnificent bracelet now is as necessary to the existence of a woman as the air she breathes.'

The fashion for centre partings, roll curls, ringlets and side curls hanging down either side of the head began in the 1820s, worn with feathers, flowers, and bands—if you couldn't grow your own curls, you were obliged to buy false ones. In a letter from Washington a Society belle pleaded, 'One thing I could not get—curls, French curls, parted on the forehead, you know how. You must get them for me, either in New York or Philadelphia. Now remember, *curls*!'

This was also the period of the gigot or leg-of-mutton sleeve which echoed the fullness of the skirt. There is a tendency for sleeves to echo the shape of the skirt but, claims Young, it is a tendency, not a rule. We have here two aspects of fashion—the independent, spontaneous dynamism of the gigot sleeves which recur naturally, and Lady Granville's concern over bracelets. The sleeve reveals how fashion has its own imperative, while Society judges the front-runners by the quality and value of their brace-lets. Fashions were given considerable impetus by the rapidly changing vogue in accessories and hairstyles. Where costumes may alter only slightly over the year, hairstyles set a brisk pace. 'The hair is dressed rather fuller in curls on the forehead than last

A pellise for outdoor wear, 1826, when the Empire line was about to give way to the bell-shaped dresses of 1830, and when sleeves were filling out. The bell skirt, wide shoulders and wide hat all serve to emphasize the narrowness of the waist, the most recurring feature in women's fashions. The lady's pellise has a wide, flat collar stretching over her shoulders and called a pelerine, she carries an 'indispensible', or purse.

Big, gigot sleeves were a major feature of sixteenth-century costume. They appeared again in the seventeenth century and remained in fashion for sixty years. They made a come-back in the 1830s as three types – the sleeve that puffed out from shoulder to elbow, gradually tapering to a tight fit at the wrist. This was the gigot or leg-of-mutton type. Another was the sleeve which ballooned from shoulder to wrist. These were called 'imbecile sleeves', from a fancied similarity to the sleeves of straight jackets. The third type was the demi-gigot which narrowed to the elbow then continued tight down the forearm to the cuff.

Hat and hairstyles for December, 1826, when 'The hair of young persons is now more ornamented with flowers . . . [and] bandeaux of pearls, with other valuable ornaments, are expected to ornament the tresses of the young at full-dress parties this winter.' Hairdressers had their work cut out fashioning elaborate topknots, or marrying false ones into the wearer's own hair.

month, and shorter at the ears,' advised *La Belle Assemblée* in 1816, 'this gives a breadth and shortness to the face which is not pleasing; the hind hair is gathered round in a Roman plait, and brought to the summit of the head.'

Through the next two decades styles became increasingly ornate. Flowers were worn, and nodding plumes of feathers. For a while black hair was fashionable, and if your hair was light coloured, you perforce had it dyed. Hats were big with floppy brims embellished with feathers. Women wore cashmere shawls, and earrings and brooches. For day wear in winter, a long overcoat or gown, sometimes lined with satin and trimmed with fur, and known as the pelisse, might be worn.

The waistline had already descended from the high line to low line in 1820. Necks were no longer bare but were covered with a large fichu. Skirts were embellished with ruching and flounces, and embroidery, especially for evening wear, of gold and silver spangles. Where white muslin had been the fabric of the classic style, the romantic dresses favoured the silk and wool mixture known as challis, a fine quality cloth printed in colours.

Men's pantaloons, drawn tight by buttoning under the instep, bowed out to the greater freedom of trousers. Trousers had come by a strange and circuitous route to be acknowledged by Regency ton; once the garment of ancient Irish Celts, *triubhas* became the traditional wear for mariners. Loose fitting, they were adopted for children's clothes in the eighteenth century and eventually found favour with adults. Striped trousers were worn with a tail coat and a top hat in the 1820s.

Making way for the Victorians

The fine art of ton, the relaxed, languid style that typified the Regency man, did not thrive well in the Victorian age to come. The Victorians had fashion, but they had little time for ton. Ton was a luxury few could afford in the mighty, industrial, empire-building age of virtue and middle-class morality. Apart from the brief seven-year reign of William IV, the Regency passed into the Victorian era, and ton survived only in the bold checked and striped trousers of the 1840s and the waistcoats of the 1850s. Ton was upheld by a few Regency survivors, such as Dickens and Disraeli, but it was hardly appropriate in a society that put aside its jacket to roll up its sleeves.

In France, by the mid nineteenth century, the Second Empire of Louis Napoleon had begun. His Court was almost as flamboyant and extravagant as that of Louis XIV. The fashions of the bourgeoisie, the parvenus, the swarming middle classes were both businesslike and architectural. Romanticism was swept under the carpet and the age of realism had begun, an age of formidable crinolines and monstrous bustles, fashions of brave statuary that well complemented the expansive ideals realized by the Crystal Palace of the Great Exhibition and the dizzy spendour of the Eiffel Tower. Its designer, Gustave Eiffel, may have taken inspiration from the structured figure of Victorian women, for this was to be the age of the corset. Said the Englishwoman's *Domestic Magazine*, 'If we could, as the American lady expressed it, be melted and poured into our stays, there would be hope for all . . .'

Chapter 4

PETTICOATS AND PROPRIETY

1840-1860

Compared with the fashions of the eighteenth and early nineteenth centuries, Victorian clothes were sombre, at least as far as the men were concerned. The Victorian prayer was not only for godliness and cleanliness (the Victorians were particularly concerned with laundering, and introduced the mangle or wringer) but, above all, for prosperity as pursued by the new professional classes. Their manners, their morals and their attire reflected these attitudes. And how else was a businessman to dress, but soberly? Commerce must be made respectable, indeed dignified, mainly, perhaps, in order to promote respect from the working classes whom industry so enthusiastically exploited—and the clothing industry was no exception.

A seamstress would probably sleep under her work-table and put in an 84-hour week, sewing from eight in the morning until midnight. 'It is not linen you're wearing out,/But human creatures' lives', wrote Thomas Hood in his 'Song of the Shirt', a bitter attack on the prevailing working conditions of the period. Respectability and propriety were the goals of those who might refer to themselves as 'the likes of us', and of the lower middle classes, immortalized as Charles Pooter in *The Diary of a Nobody*, who 'bought a pair of lavender kid gloves and two white ties, in case one got spoiled in the tying.'

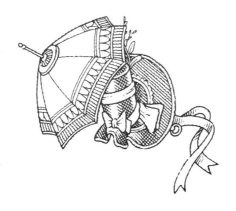

Acknowledging our expansion into a consumer society, the eighteenth century political economist Adam Smith, in his celebrated work *The Wealth of Nations*, said that 'To found a great empire for the sole purpose of raising up a people of customers may at first sight appear a project fit only for a nation of shopkeepers. It is, however, a project altogether unfit for a nation of shopkeepers; but extremely fit for a nation whose Government is influenced by shopkeepers.'

If we were not a nation of shopkeepers it is certain that we were a nation of shoemakers, a handicraft trade whose customers were the best shod in Europe. The first national census had been taken in 1801 and did not cover trades, but the second in 1831 gave the population of the country as a whole, and that of the separate counties, including the principal trades. Top of the list came the shoemakers. In wool-wealthy Devon, for example, there were 4253 out of a population of 494,000.

In London there were an astonishing 15,000 shoemakers and 13,000 tailors—the figure did not include the shoemakers' apprentices, journeymen and 'shoemakers' wives', nor the clog-makers, nor the retail shoe shops such as Lilley & Skinner's (founded in 1842), nor the army of outworkers employed by wholesale manufacturers, many of these outworkers being women and children.

To provide footwear for the few hundred of the aristocracy, the 170,000 of the persons of property—i.e. the gentry—and the 420,000 members of the professional class, not to mention the merchants, English shoemakers crouched over their lasts to stitch Wellington boots (one guinea per pair), Blücher boots, Hessian boots, Clarence boots, Congress boots, and a wide variety of shoes. By mid century there were twenty million people in Britain, and the majority were wearing boots, especially 'the lower orders, such as jockeys, grooms and butlers'.

The leather boot popularized by the Duke of Wellington (and also worn by Napoleon) went out of fashion for a time, although it and the Hessian boot (named not from the fabric, but from Hesse in Germany) survived in America, while the boot named after Wellington's ally, Field Marshal Blücher, a 'high-low' ankle boot, remained a basic type throughout the century. Wellingtons are still with us today, of course, only now made of rubber and available in green. Apart from Society, boots were worn by countrymen, 'bought with the extra money the men earned in the harvest field,' wrote Flora Thompson in *Lark Rise to Candleford*, 'nobody went barefoot, even though some of the toes might sometimes stick out.' In the North of England, and throughout France, people wore wooden clogs. Even when galoshes were introduced the soles remained of wood.

Dainty shoes and Balmoral boots

Women were expected to possess dainty feet, and to fit them into dainty shoes. 'There scarcely exists an Englishwoman whose toes are not folded one over the other', warned *The Handbook to the Toilet* in 1841 'each of these crooked, and their nails almost destroyed. From childhood the rage for tight shoes and small feet exists.' While men were allowed large, practical hands and feet,

Men's boots were of three main types—the top boot, where the top turned over and was usually a different colour to the rest of the boot; the Hessian, where the top edge went to a point from which a tassel was suspended; and the Blücher, a lace-up short boot. The Wellington was a type of top boot but without the turnover.

women—or rather ladies—by contrast and in proportion to their smaller frames, fitted their hands into slim gloves and their feet into heel-less satin shoes and slippers—you see them peeping out demurely from beneath the petticoats and dresses in the fashion plates of the period. They had been introduced from Paris, in plain black, in the 1820s and were *de rigueur* for thirty years.

There is undoubtedly an unconscious, erotic element in tightness, both in corsets as well as shoes, but there is also the consideration of proportion, even though the feet may be for the most part hidden beneath a large crinoline. By mid century women had taken to wearing boots, laced and elastic-sided, such as the popular 'Balmoral' boot, with patent leather trimmings, as worn by Queen Victoria, and designed by Sparkes Hall of Regent Street. Boots were already being fitted with india-rubber soles, an American invention along with rubber galoshes; American technology was going to strike hard at our nation of shoemakers.

With the Declaration of Independence the Americans had gained, among other things, independence from English shoe-makers, although their skills were needed in the New World. This state of affairs, with the pioneers clad in shoddy footwear for lack of expertise, had induced manufacturers to seek fast and efficient ways of machine production. Accordingly, the Blake machine for sewing on soles followed hard on the heels of a method where the soles were fitted to the uppers by wooden pegs, and another where shoes were welded by the Goodyear process. The mass-produced shoe, both in England and in America, bore no comparison to the hand-made 'bespoke' item of the early nineteenth centry. In those days there were no right and left shoes for the working classes, nor for the military: some regiments had to wear their boots 'on alternate feet on alternate days'.

But with perseverance, American techniques improved to such an extent that by the 1870s they were able to challenge the supremacy of the French shoe designers, the Americans offering a broad shoe, the French a narrow, pointed-toe shoe. Not surprisingly, the most fashion-conscious wearers opted for the pointed shoe and suffered the discomfort. I remember a colleague who forced his feet into pointed 'winkle-pickers'. He winced at every step, but defended his shoes, saying, 'I'll do *anything* to be in fashion . . .'

The ultimate in nineteenth century femininity. A promenade dress from La Belle Assemblée, *1840. It is described as a 'robe of rose organdie, a low corsage rounded at the top, drawn in full at the waist and trimmed with lace. The hat, a* Gros d'Afrique chapeau, *is decorated with scarlet blossoms and foliage.'*

Conformity off the peg

The fashions of the Victorian era were those of a successful industrial society which at times contrasted oddly with the agrarian traditions. French art critic Francis Wey, visiting London in the 1850s, was astonished by the size and activity of London society, where during the weekday afternoons 40,000 private carriages were driven about the streets and in the parks. In Hyde Park, on a Tuesday afternoon Wey saw, 'Two or three thousand women strolling over the lawns and under the splendid lime trees, beeches and oaks . . . Groups of friends were sitting on the chairs or squatting on the grass. A flock of sheep fatter than any known to us grazed peacefully and cows ruminated with philosophical detachment in the midst of the crowd. It is a unique experience, in

the heart of a great city to wander about woods and meadows and embrace at a glance pompous equipages with powdered footmen and rustic herds of cows, goats and sheep with elegant ladies trailing silks and laces among them.'

Where the silks and satins, wigs and jewels of the eighteenth century were the expression of the privilege and wealth enjoyed by the minority, the Victorian employers and employees alike dressed in deference to industry. They did so even in France, and the dull uniformity of men's clothes in particular may be due in part to the emergence of the 'ready-made' tailoring shops.

The first of these, Coutard in Paris, supplied the bourgeoisie with off-the-peg suits that were far lower in price than bespoke suits from the traditional tailor, and were monotonously respectable, 'It is excessively simple to explain the triumph of this fashion in terms of the progressive democratization of the Western world,' said historian Theodore Zeldin in 1977, 'the universal black suit denoted not so much the triumph of democracy, so much as a new form of social distinction.'

But it probably had more to do with the conformity of commerce. 'The tendency to cling to established forms with the minimum amount of yearly change,' says Agnes Young, 'seems clearly a pronounced feature of masculine clothes that has no counterpart in women's fashions.' Until the mid eighteenth century, men's clothes were notable for their sartorial flamboyance. As trade developed and a new middle class appeared, men turned from the doublet and hose to the uniformity of coat, waistcoat and breeches. By the mid nineteenth century colour and decoration had almost entirely given way to achromatic sobriety.

The reasons are not hard to find. Finance, law, medicine and education are serious businesses commanding respect and trust which is equated with a conservative and dignified appearance. We may suspect men who wear unorthodox attire, especially those in professions that trade upon sincerity—this is why newspaper editors and editorial staff, and the directors of advertising agencies wear suits, collars and ties. In Frederick Wakeman's novel about American advertising, *The Hucksters*, the hero Vic, before going to an interview, selects with great care 'a damned sincere tie'.

The universal suit could be easily adapted to the mass-market, and ready-mades produced a 'caste uniform' for gentlemen. Conformity was required and obtained, as was the ban on sartorial provocativeness, which suggests to Zeldin that 'The age of the black suit coincided more exactly with the age of sexual inhibitions than with that of democracy.'

Solidity with a firm foundation

The presumed stern sexual morality of the Victorians has been the subject of much speculation and debate. Later generations have decided that the voluminous petticoats, corsets and crinolines of the women, and the sombre, utilitarian 'uniforms' of the men must perforce have been sexually inhibiting and were the expression of moral repression. In other words, if the stiff and much encumbered figure of the Victorian woman implies frigidity she must, *ipso facto*, be frigid. It is further suggested that women's

Country wear in 1844 from the French magazine Le Moniteur de la Mode. *Children's clothes generally imitated adult fashions—girls even wore corsets and petticoats. The lady carries a pagoda parasol, an essential accessory to shield her delicate complexion from the sun. Many parasols had carved ivory handles and ferrules, and the covers were trimmed with Maltese lace and fringed borders.*

clothes, which were certainly physically restricting, could symbolize masculine domination. They were the object of endless satire from the press and the cartoonists of *Punch*.

'Woman has been a slave rather than the mistress of her costume,' said the fashion historian Willett Cunnington, and he added that dress, 'turns Woman into an artist and Man into an art critic. And the Englishwoman's costume is, after all, completely successful in that it provokes endless criticism.' The male attitude to women's dress, often one of amused tolerance, drew sharp comment from the fashion journalist Mrs Eric Pritchard, 'What utter rubbish it is for the ordinary man, and particularly an Englishman, to attempt to criticize woman in matters of dress!'

The Victorian woman, far from being truly emancipated and bound to conform to the strict rules of society, was as preoccupied with matters of dress as time and her allowance would permit. Fashion may have been to many women a refuge and afforded a degree of autonomy, although opinions on the corset were sharply divided. In her *Period Piece*, author Gwen Raverat recalled that, 'We did rebel against stays. Margaret says that the first time she was put into them—when she was about thirteen—she ran round and round the nursery screaming with rage. I did not do that. I simply went and took them off; endured the sullen row which ensued, when my soft-shelled condition was discovered; was forcibly re-corseted; and, as soon as possible went away and took them off again . . .'

The essence of the modes of the Victorians, with their boots and corsets and crinolines, was that of solidity—solidity with a firm foundation. The bell-shaped cycle reached its zenith in the huge skirts of the period and was helped perhaps by several pragmatic factors. One of these was the introduction of the sewing machine, which encouraged the use of the abundance of material made available by the booming textile industry. Furthermore, the volume of fabric (in some dresses as much as 48 yards) needed for a 'full-blown' crinoline dress was a testimony to this age of progress and plenty and democracy—both the mistress and her maids wore crinolines.

Yet do not imagine for one moment that uniformity of dress in both sexes had finally demoted status. Many working people wore clothes that were cast-offs or 'hand-me-downs' from their employers, or were purchased from second-hand clothes dealers. As for the woman of Society, 'every cap, bow, streamer, ruffle, fringe, bustle, glove and other elaboration symbolized some status category for the female wearer, mourning dress being the quintescence of this demarcation.' Sociologist Leonore Davidoff, in her study of *The Best Circles*, went on to describe a footman, with long experience of upper-class households, remembering that 'jewellery was a badge that women wore like a sergeant-major's stripes or a field marshal's baton, it showed achievement, rank, position.' It is not surprising, then, that girls and women of all classes were preoccupied with dress.

Fashion becomes a mighty industry

London was, and had been since the eighteenth century, the capital of men's fashions, with Paris dominating the fashions for women's clothes. Men's clothes were made by tailors, their hats by hatters, while women's clothes were the province of 'mantua makers' (a term surviving from the past century), seamstresses and milliners. Strictly speaking, a milliner was one who sold ribbons and trimmings, especially of silk, imported from Milan; later a milliner made hats exclusively, while the importer of dress accessories was a haberdasher. By the time of the aforementioned census in 1831 there were three thousand haberdashers in London, nine fan-makers, three hundred lace-makers, and a thousand old-clothes dealers. The population was just over one million, and 13 per cent of the workforce were employed in the fashion industry—nine per cent being women.

Amelia Bloomer

Mrs Amelia J. Bloomer of Seneca Falls, New York, wearing her famous garment in 1850. In her brave attempt to introduce dress reform, she urged women to rebel against the cumbersome crinoline, and adopt her oriental-style trousers, to be worn under a short frock. As James Laver has pointed out, the style was by no means unfeminine. But it was highly controversial and provoked hostility in Victorian men when she visited England. They felt their authority would be threatened, and their masculinity undermined, if women wore trousers. 'Bloomers' were to come into their own in the 1880s, however, when they proved ideal for the adventurous woman cyclist.

Demure femininity, 1844, exemplified by copious skirts, slender waists, flowers, frills, ringlet curls and pretty bonnets. The woman on the right wears a pelisse robe or redingote for outdoor attire, and a long, striped Albanian scarf or shawl. The nineteenth century was the age of the shawl, especially Kashmir or Paisley, and the fashionable lady had a wide selection in her wardrobe. The Empress Josephine reputedly had four hundred, which she had to replace regularly as Napoleon was in the habit of snatching them from her shoulders and throwing them on the fire . . .

Modes de Paris.
Petit Courrier des Dames.

Dress also seems to have been the preoccupation of industry. Of the urban trades, after the shoemakers came the tailors, followed by the haberdashers, while competing for fourth place came the hairdressers and jewellers—by mid century there were 2600 jewellers in London. Even in the provinces a city such as York boasted as many as 950 dressmakers and seamstresses, to clothe 10,000 women of the city who might be able to afford at least one dress per season. The textile industry, notorious for the exploitation of women and children, even after the Factory Act came into force, employed well over a million persons, not to mention the fact that 'great numbers in the domestic class are partially employed in making, mending and washing dresses'.

In the 1860s there were nearly a million domestic servants in Britain, of which 100,000 were housemaids. Practically all of them made their own clothes, or bought dresses second-hand from the Irish and Jewish dealers, and made the necessary alterations. Fashions were followed if the wearer could afford them, housemaids and factory girls wearing modest crinolines, if the home or factory permitted them. But many did not. 'The present ugly fashion of HOOPS, or CRINOLINE, as it is called, is, however, quite unfitted for work in our factories,' warned Courtauld's Mills in 1860. 'Among the Power Looms it is almost impossible, and highly dangerous; among the Winding and Drawing Engines it greatly impedes the passage of Overseers, Wasters, etc., and is inconvenient to all. At the Mills it is equally inconvenient, and still more mischievous, by bringing the dress against the Spindles, while also it sometimes becomes shockingly indecent when the young people are standing upon the Sliders.'

It was a mighty industry. In the cotton and wool industries were dealers, dyers and brokers in addition to the three hundred separate occupations in the factories themselves. The cotton workers turned out—night and day—bales of brocade, calico, muslin, coutil, poplin, nankeen, fustian, dimity, chintz, batiste, velvet, tarlatan, piqué and georgette. From the wool factories came beaver, cashmere, broadcloth, challis, felt, merino, tweed and voile and worsted. As for the silk industry, even the domestic servants had a silk dress for 'best' wear. The middle class and above wore their silk dresses for evening engagements, also for street wear.

If it were possible to exploit a silkworm, then you can be sure they were working overtime to provide the fabric. But in fact the silkworm is killed in order to obtain the thread, which was worked by hand and spun on looms—there were said to be 17,000 looms in the silk centre of Spitalfields—mainly to produce damask and brocade.

The retail outlets kept pace with productivity. One of the first department stores was Bon Marché in Paris in the 1850s, but one respected fashion journalist and historian Alison Adburgham, in her splendid book *Shops and Shopping*, shows that the first of the many great department stores were those of Kendal, Milne & Faulkner ('Silk & Shawl Warehousemen and General Drapers') in Manchester, and Bainbridge's of Newcastle-upon-Tyne, both in 1830. It seems that they were not before time. 'By mid century onwards, the number of drapery shops which were expanding into considerable stores was so great that it is possible to mention only a few.' They are now household names to the British at home, and to visitors from abroad: John Lewis, Peter Robinson, Dickens & Jones, Swan & Edgar (no more), Marshall & Snelgrove. Drapers carried large stocks of fabrics, from which a lady could make her choice for a dress. She would then purchase sufficient lengths of material to take to her dressmaker.

A jacket or paletot, worn in 1870, about the time that the polonaise *style was once again popular. Materials were silk, faille, velvet and* gros grain.

Since Victoria had come to the throne, an increased and increasing population was matched by increased literacy. A by-product of the fashion industry included the printing and publishing of fashion magazines, women's interest magazines, and a vast number of books and booklets on dressmaking and pattern-cutting. There is no other industry, apart perhaps from undertaking, that has had so dramatic an increase as the world of fashion, and the two were in the Victorian era mutually inclusive, in view of the rigid rules of contemporary etiquette regarding mourning dress.

'First mourning,' writes Leonore Davidoff, 'was worn for a year and a day. This meant black clothes covered with crêpe, no ornaments and a widow's cap with veil. Second mourning lasted for the next twelve months, black with less crêpe, without a cap and jet ornaments only, called "slighting" the mourning. The third year was half mourning when grey or mauve could be added for colour . . . The very act of producing correct mourning—in dress and its accessories, in stationery, seals, floral decorations and other insignia—indicated not just the material basis to invest in all this equipment but that the woman was sufficiently initiated into the mysteries of proper mourning to carry it off.'

What one is seen to do and what one is seen to wear had to be right. If you did not observe what was in fashion from your contemporaries, the magazines carried the latest bulletins from Paris. Even so, in those days fashions evolved slowly, modifications occurring mainly in the sleeves and the height of the corsage, the addition of flounces and lace trimmings, and with such accessories as shawls and bonnets. Bonnets were worn throughout the 1840s, close fitting and following the shape of the face, emphasizing the demure, submissive look.

They were not called bonnets, however, but *chapeaux* or *capote*, the latter were generally longer and in a straight line from crown to brim. 'I may cite two of the prettiest *capotes* for the demi-toilette that I have seen for a long time,' wrote the fashion correspondent of *La Belle Assemblée* rapturously. 'They have been ordered for two sisters distinguished as leaders of fashion: these *capotes* are composed of bands of white satin and white *velours épinglé* alternately. The exterior is decorated with a *quirlande* of white and rose-coloured shaded marabouts, and the interior with *mancinis* composed of small moss roses half-blown.'

Clothes were made to be worn for several seasons, perhaps several years, and there is not a great deal of difference between the fashions of, say, 1840 and those of 1848. Because of the quantities of fabric used, dresses were expensive and complicated to make, and had to be ordered well in advance if they were to be worn for a special event. Silk dresses, especially, were always lined so that the silk fabric could later be stripped from the lining, turned, and used for a different pattern, or a similar style, employing the unfaded face of the recycled material.

Every girl knew how to ply a needle and thread and was able at least to attend to running repairs. Educated young ladies could follow the fashion news in *La Belle Assemblée* or the *Lady's Magazine*, or when in Paris catch up on the latest *Petit Courriere des Dames*. There were also the fashion correspondents who sent bulletins from the Faubourg St Honoré with such inspiring stuff as, 'Our season promises to be a very brilliant one, indeed, the luxury of dress goes on increasing so rapidly, that we shall soon want sumptuary laws to put a stop to it.'

Highland Fever – Tartan becomes big business

'Luxury of dress' referred mainly to the wealth of materials available, since manufacturers could and did produce a wide range of fabrics and designs, in particular the cotton and silk industries. One of the most successful—perhaps *the* most successful fabric

Evening dress from the 1840s featured in Le Moniteur de la Mode. *The* décolletage *was either cut square across, or dipped down to the cleavage when it was known as* en coeur. *A further embellishment would be a lace frill or 'bertha' which covered the bosom and short sleeves. Older women covered their bare shoulders with a lace fichu or shawl.*

LE MONITEUR DE LA MODE.
Journal du Grand Monde
Edition du Journal spécial de la Maison
Popelin Ducarre, rue Neuve Vivienne 41.
Bonnet de chez Barenne & Cᵉ fleurs de Constantin.
Bureaux du Journal, 15, Boulevart Montmartre, à Paris.

Published by Chowne Gosselin & Cᵉ.
265. Regent Street. London.

Published by E. Gambart & Junin
12 Dennemark Stᵗ Soho London.

THE PASSION FOR FASHION

Scottish ladies wore the tartan of their family, or their husband's clan. Lady Scott, in this portrait by Sir William Beechey (1744–1854), wears in her hat the tartan of the Scotts, a Border clan.

design in fashion history — is that of tartan plaid. The permutations of pattern and colour seem limitless and adaptable to almost any fabric. The Celtic revival or 'Highland Fever' had begun with George IV's visit to Edinburgh in 1882, an event organized by Sir Walter Scott, during which the King appeared dressed in Royal Stewart tartan — certainly the first Hanoverian ever to wear the kilt.

The widespread popularity of Scott's Waverley novels, and the romantic portraits of Highland chieftains swamped in tartan plaid, by David Wilkie and Sir Henry Raeburn, gave considerable impetus to the output of the Scottish mills, recently mechanized by the advances of the Industrial Revolution. Tartan was suddenly big business, and the provenance of several 'ancient' tartans may date from this period. In order to establish some clan pedigrees, James Logan wrote *The Scottish Gael* in 1831, in which he established rightly or wrongly the existence of 55 different setts, or tartans.

Perhaps inspired by Logan's book, two Glasgow tailors came south to London in 1838 and opened a tweed and tartan shop in Aldgate. They later moved premises to Knightsbridge, and their shop, The Scotch House, is still there, the success and popularity of tartan now expanded to an archive of 350 — unsurpassed. The French, from their association with the 'Auld Alliance', took to the tartan wholeheartedly, and fresh impetus was given when Queen Victoria rebuilt Balmoral, her residence in the Highlands, which became ablaze with tartans from floor to ceiling. Tweed manufacturers were carried along on the wave of enthusiasm and began to promote check cloth which was ideally suited to menswear, trousers especially.

While the Scottish mills had the monopoly, there was no patent for tartans, and the French silk looms in Lyon began production of some delicate and beautiful silk plaids—so fine that they could be drawn, like cashmere shawls, through a wedding ring. In France, industrialization produced cheaper textiles. Shawls, worn by every fashionable lady, were expensive until 1850, when the mills of Rheims began mass-producing tartan shawls in wool, when prices promptly dropped from 450 francs to eight francs per shawl. The French may be credited for pioneering the use of tartans as a fashion accessory, noted by the Paris correspondent of *La Belle Assemblée*, 'At the Tuileries we see nothing but sashes, and they are generally of Scottish plaid. Young, old, handsome, ugly, straight, crooked, humpbacked, tall, short, squint-eyed, one-eyed, black-eyed, grey-eyed, flaxen-headed, everyone had a sash tied in a bow behind, the long ends hanging at her heels, or the long ends streaming in the wind.'

Huge quantities of underwear

Although the mid nineteenth century is now regarded as the period of corsets and crinolines and bustles, of thrift and modesty and propriety, the Victorians were the pioneers of a further enduring gift to the inventory of fashion—underwear. Not in tartan, perhaps, but in linen, cotton, muslin, calico, lace and silk. According to legend, Queen Victoria decreed that women should start wearing knickers, or rather drawers, as they were then known. Drawers pre-dated the Victorians though, and were uncharacteristically immodest, in that they were open down the inside seams, being secured only at the waist and legs which ended well below the knee.

One might well ask why the Victorians developed under-clothing when women had survived for thousands of years in a world innocent of lingerie. For one thing, underclothes were inevitable and would have occurred sooner or later in a society preoccupied by changing fashions in dress. For another, the Victorians were aware of the needs of hygiene, for was it not an adjunct of piety, according to Wesley? '. . . slovenliness is no part of religion; that neither this nor any text of Scripture, condemns neatness of apparel. Certainly this is a duty, not a sin. Cleanliness is, indeed, next to godliness.'

In *Crinolines and Crimping Irons*, a thorough study of Victorian cleaning methods, the authors Walkley and Foster explain that Victorian dresses suffered very little from body dirt. 'This was chiefly because of the huge quantities of underwear worn. A dress worn over a chemise, a camisole, and several petticoats, was effectively protected from contact with the body.' If underclothes were at first utilitarian, they soon acquired an erotic (and French) identity as lingerie. The facility of the sewing machine, pioneered by French, English and American designers, and rendered domestically practicable by Isaac Singer, from 1850 onwards, made it possible for women to add frills and laces to their underwear.

The novelist Sir Walter Scott was mainly responsible for inspiring the fashion for tartan outside Scotland, and it was taken up enthusiastically—then as now—by the French.

LES VICTIMES DE LA MODE, PAR BERTALL (SUITE). — *Essai sur les beautés de la crinoline.*

(VOIR LE N° 1118.

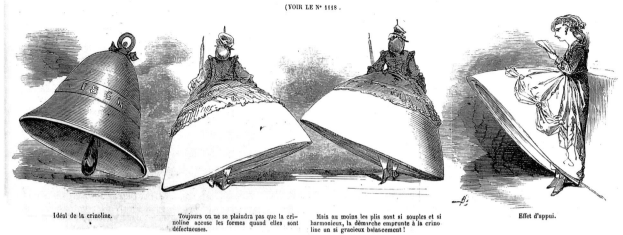

Idéal de la crinoline.

Toujours on ne se plaindra pas que la crinoline accuse les formes quand elles sont défectueuses.

Mais au moins les plis sont si souples et si harmonieux, la démarche emprunte à la crinoline un si gracieux balancement !

Effet d'appui.

Effet de porte.

Chinoiserie.

Effet de marche.

Femme perfectionnée en 1864. Le triangle a toujours personnifié la perfection. — Problème de géométrie : étant donné le triangle ABC, déterminer au juste la position que Madame occupe dans le triangle.

The crinoline was consistently parodied by cartoonists. ABOVE and OPPOSITE, the problems of travel and of passing through doorways, and the risk of catching fire are here jocularly recorded by the French cartoonist Bertall. The men, for their part, saw their own attire as perfectly normal, but James Laver decided that, 'A visitor from Mars contemplating a man in a frock coat and top hat and a woman in a crinoline might well have supposed they belonged to different species.'

The erotic nature of underwear is precisely due to the non-utilitarian embroidery, the more so since lingerie remains hidden beneath the outer garments. Moreover, underwear was invested with a somewhat gratuitous erotic quality by the Victorians themselves. 'Dare I whisper', wrote Mrs Eric Pritchard provocatively, 'of a strong fancy among many immaculate people for black undergarments? This affectation is chiefly noticeable amongst Americans. There is something curiously effective about black silk, silk gauze, or finest cambric, trimmed with beautiful white lace.' Mrs Pritchard, securing for herself a degree of respectability by using her married name was, in fact, a respected fashion journalist writing at the turn of the century and greatly encouraged marital bliss among her readers, with the help of lingerie, '. . . the woman possessed of the laudable desire to appear lovely in her husband's eyes will not fail, if she be wise in her generation, to give this part of her wardrobe careful consideration.'

Underclothes were among the first garments to be sold, ready-made, over the counter, and no doubt some manufacturers realized that embroidery would enhance sales as well as the figure; lingerie was bound sooner or later to appropriate some of the froth and tumble of lace, satin frills, and broderie anglaise borders long displayed by dresses, petticoats and bonnets.

What did the Victorian lady wear, exactly? A chemise, sleeveless, round-necked and embroidered, and reaching down below the knee was the first layer. The chemise was tucked into the drawers, and since this realized much surplus material, the natural development was to unite the two, and thus combinations or 'combs' were born. Over the chemise was worn the corset or stays, then the petticoat.

When the horsehair crinoline gave way to the hooped crinoline, made of a steel, wood or whalebone frame, petticoats might be worn over the hoop to disguise the structure. That the entire thing was highly inflammable was widely acknowledged, although garments could be made fireproof, and it is a fact that many women died in the cause of fashion. In his *The Life of Oscar Wilde*, Hesketh Pearson recalled how Sir William Wilde, Oscar's father, lost his two 'natural' daughters 'when the crinoline of one caught fire at a dance, and ignited that of the other who tried to save her.'

The crinoline had, however, the advantage of liberating women from the many layers of petticoats needed to maintain the bell-shaped profile. The crinoline was simply a cage, tied around the waist. The structure was made of fine steel hoops increasing in circumference from waist to a frill at the bottom, which was usually made of horsehair, from which the crinoline (French *crin* for horsehair) gets its name. The design was collapsible so that the wearer could sit down or pass through spaces narrower than the crinoline would seem to allow.

As an item of underwear, it is certainly the one most ridiculed and maligned, especially by the press, and often by its wearers too. Queen Victoria refused to wear one and begged the ladies of England to oppose the fashion of the 'indelicate, expensive, dangerous and hideous article called Crinoline'. Others

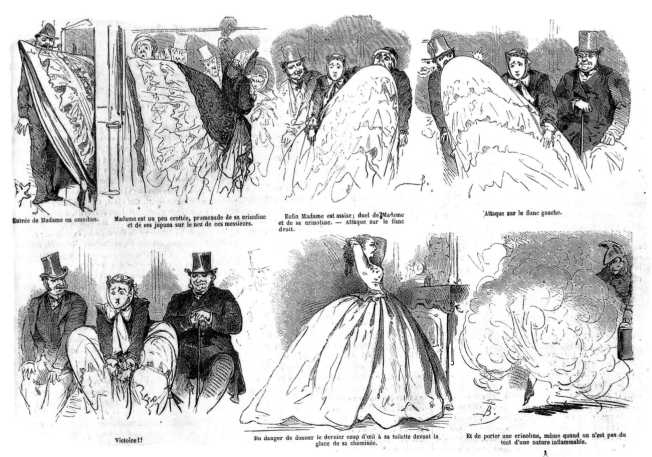

Entrée de Madame en omnibus.

Madame est un peu crottée, promenade de sa crinoline et de ses jupons sur le nez de ces messieurs.

Enfin Madame est assise; duel de Madame et de sa crinoline. — Attaque sur le flanc droit.

Attaque sur le flanc gauche.

Victoire!!

Du danger de donner le dernier coup d'œil à sa toilette devant la glace de sa cheminée.

Et de porter une crinoline, même quand on n'est pas du tout d'une nature inflammable.

Berthas, braces, cazenous and fichus were some of the essential accessories in the fashionable wardrobe of the mid nineteenth century. The sewing machine and the workforce of poorly paid seamstresses created both demand and supply.

lamented its passing: Owen Raverat, previously quoted, asked her Aunt Etty what it was like to wear one. 'Oh, it was delightful,' she said, 'I've never been so comfortable since they went out. It kept your petticoats away from your legs, and made walking so light and easy.'

Far more controversial was the corset. This curved, shaped, sculpted and engineered undergarment has attracted the serious attention of the medical profession, sociologists, reformers (who may also be sociologists), psychoanalysts, historians, fashion writers, artists, couturiers, and the wearers themselves. The corset defines the ideal body shape and was worn by all classes of women regardless of whether or not they had an ideal body shape; the corset was ubiquitous and worn by all and sundry—schoolgirls not excepted.

The leading question was why? The question seems pertinent in view of the fact that corsets were said to be uncomfortable, even permanently damaging, yet they were in constant demand and manufacturers competed in the subtlety of their engineering and delicacy of their decoration and embellishment. By mid century there were 10,000 corset-makers in Paris, and the same number in London. By 1890 the number had more than doubled, emphasizing the value wearers put on this singular garment. Many women made their own corsets at home, from patterns in ladies' magazines and fashion journals. Before the domestic sewing machine, stay-making had been a man's job, because it needed strong fingers to stitch through the stout fabric.

Throughout history, and especially during the eighteenth and nineteenth centuries, the ideal of beauty has been concentrated on shape and form. The curve, the roundness and softness of the female body is shared and appreciated by most races. In Western society the ideal feminine shape, until the 1920s, was one that emphasized the curves of the body and in particular the waist, hips, bust and shoulders—a narrow waist had priority over all. Where other features might be modest and unassuming, a shapely figure could more than compensate. The desirable 'hourglass' figure reflected youthfulness, while giving prominence to the hips below and the bust above, and thereby the principal female functions. The correlation of youthfulness and potency were two reasons for the continued success of the corset.

The literature of the corset is vast, especially in France where several academic studies appeared, notably *Le Corset* by Dr O'Followell in 1905, another by Leoty in 1893. Regular campaigns were mounted against the evils of 'Fashion & Deformity' and the awful effects of 'Tight Lacing', but they were largely ignored.

Marvels of structure and symmetry

In any event, it seems that the ill-effects caused by corsets may well have been exaggerated. Valerie Steele, in *Fashion and Eroticism* is cautious about reports relating the corset to deformity. 'Corsets probably neither supported the spine nor deformed it, although both of these beliefs indicate fears about the essential weakness of the body. The stories of crushed ribs—let alone deliberately removed ribs—have yet to be authenticated; there are some female skeletons from the 1880s at the Smithsonian Institu-

tion with what appear to be deformed ribs. Corsets probably did cause some health problems. The restriction of the chest led to upper diaphragmatic breathing, while the constriction of the waist and abdomen probably caused digestive problems, such as constipation.'

A corset may be constructed of a dozen or more separate panels shaped to the waist, and made with the twilled cotton fabric coutil, lined and perhaps quilted. In the 1870s corsets became greatly varied in style and design when the crinoline gave way to the bustle, since the hips were now revealed as part of the body

Paris fashions featured in the Italian magazine Corriere delle Dame *in 1863, when the crinoline reached its most fullsome proportions. Victorian clothes, with their acres of heavy cloth and miles of ribbons and flounces, were created at the expense of thousands of sweated dressmakers.*

73

In the 1860s a carriage, or visiting, dress would have had a substantial train which dragged heavily in the dust and mud. Skirts could be hoisted to avoid fouling them by means of cords run through a shirr along the hem and up through the waistband. In the United States this device was known as an 'elevator', and was worn with a 'cage americaine' which raised the hoops of the crinoline.

line. Some of these new corsets were marvels of structure and symmetry, with up to twenty panels and gussets, whalebones or steel reinforcers (the whale population being seriously depleted), plus a spoon-shaped busk. The busk was a long stiffener that could be inserted in a sheath down the front of the corset to keep the torso rigid and upright. Later in the century corsets became increasingly decorative, with facings of silk and satin and embroidered with lace and bows.

There were over eleven million women in mid Victorian England, and for the majority there was no alternative to the corset and crinoline. Since crinolines were banned in the mills of the North, girls would wear printed cotton dresses and large shawls, but many kept their corsets or stays (stays are shorter and simpler than corsets but are, like corsets, laced up at the back). Elsewhere the uniform of all classes preserved the bell-shaped

dress irrespective of inconvenience. 'The dresses of the bell cycle,' said Agnes Young, 'were, in and of themselves, among the most amazing that fashion has ever produced. They were incredibly big and cumbersome, and restricted literally every movement the wearer chose to make.'

Even so, the pioneer spirit of the women remained undaunted. In America, the homesteaders 'trailed their petticoats across the prairies, and though living a life of hardship, never relinquished their fantastic garments.' Not a few Victorian women responded to the spirit of adventure or duty—or both. Fanny Duberly, for example, the wife of Captain Henry Duberly of the 8th Hussars was the only officer's wife to witness the campaign in the Crimea. It is likely that both Fanny *and* her husband wore corsets, at a time when the cavalry was so rigidly shaped by their uniforms that officers could 'scarce raise their sword arm'.

'For the pleasure of being smart'

The redoubtable Fanny wrote to her sister Selina from the field of battle. 'This is my walking costume for going up and down ship's sides—holding on by the ropes—tumbling in and out of boats—and waddling through the knee-deep mud—I can wear no other—as to a bonnet I can never stand one again.' But Fanny kept her stays on, and wrote again to Selina requesting 'twelve staylaces' plus 'three shifts, two very thick flannel petticoats in readiness for the winter, a warm dark gown and warm stockings . . . a warm thick winter gown, woollen or plaid, with velvet or other trimming for the body. The skirt to be made up quite plain, not exorbitantly expensive, full and lined.' Fashion was a priority even in the Crimea, and Fanny goes on to request, 'A black wideawake hat, low-crowned and pretty. Also three yards of black ribbon velvet and a plume of cock's hackle and an ostrich feather, also black. I can trim the hat when it comes.'

In the 1860s the bell-shaped skirt began to narrow and take on an appearance that would lead to the bustle, the back-fullness cycle that was to remain until the end of the century. The fall of the 'amazing' crinoline was bound to occur, but did it fall or was it pushed? Legend has it that one person alone was responsible for the demise of the crinoline, and the introduction of the bustle, a person who was to have a profound influence on the history of modern fashion—the first, and some claim the greatest, couturier, Charles Frederick Worth. It is unlikely that Worth alone was responsible for the timely arrival of the new shape, but he gave it a nudge in the right direction, and he also gave it style.

By modern standards, many of Worth's creations seem over-dressed, but at the height of the Victorian era, when Worth became the 'supreme arbiter of taste in dress' the richness of your attire still proclaimed social status or, if you were one of the *nouveaux riches*, your wealth. The couturier had arrived, and would revolutionize the dress industry. From now on, uniformity would give way to exclusivity for the few, and imitation by the many. The fashionable women of the *haut monde* would turn to the *haut couturier* for, as Worth himself put it, 'the pleasure of being smart, and for the greater joy of snuffing out the competition from other women . . .'

Fanny Duberly, in a sketch accompanying a letter to her sister Selina, from the Crimea in 1855. 'This is my walking costume for going up and down ship's sides,' she writes, 'holding on by ropes—tumbling in and out of boats.' She hoists her skirts away from the mud and wears a flat straw hat. 'As to a bonnet, I can never stand one again.'

Chapter 5

ENTER THE COUTURIER
1860-1900

The mid Victorian period and the Second Empire in France witnessed a new phenomenon in fashion—the couturier—a role more or less invented by Charles Frederick Worth. Here was a man, or 'man-milliner' as some called him, who actually dictated what women should wear—even the Empress herself. Worth had hit upon a profound truth, that the majority of people want to follow fashion and be dictated to by an authority and arbiter of taste. Fashion had been lacking in direction but here was someone who could pull it together, and give it interest and excitement. The introduction of the dressmaking house, or salon, coincided with the expansion of the retail dress business, and the stores paid for the privilege of copying originals, copies that would be worn from Paris to San Francisco, from New York to Buenos Aires.

Couture arrived as the extravagance of the crinoline was reaching its height—or rather its width—in the 1850s. The crinoline was just one expression of fashion's recurring cycles which couture, in time, would subvert. Fashion must always be seen to be innovative, and while the Victorian man in his dark, commercial suit might be the provider of the clothes that women wore, it was the women who were the natural catalysts of style and, as some would aver, the victims of hemlines and waistlines.

The man who invented haute couture, *Charles Frederick Worth. The appointment of Worth & Bobergh as imperial dressmakers to the Empress Eugénie caused a scandal. Even a seasoned social observer such as Charles Dickens was moved to write that 'There are bearded milliners— man milliners . . . who, with their solid fingers, take the exact dimensions of the highest titled women in Paris—robe them, unrobe them, and make them turn backward and forward before them.'*

Until Worth began designing clothes for women, fashions were largely uninspired and advanced at a leisurely pace; the sewing machine was still a novelty and everything had to be stitched by hand, the *couturières* —the dressmakers—made modest developments according to the whims of their clients, their choice of fabrics, and the current fancies in the air. Yet there was little spontaneity, and although Paris was the traditional hub of women's fashions, there was nowhere else to look to, London remaining the capital of fashions for men. Fashion reports in the leading magazines were mainly based on what the ladies of Society were seen wearing at Longchamps, or at the Tuileries Ball but there was no one style.

There were fashion magazines and fashion artists, and what was currently the ton was probably arrived at by common consent in the editorial offices. Styles were drawn up, idealized of course, as an inspiration to the readers. On a more practical level, there were the paper patterns of dresses as templates for suitable fabrics to be bought from the drapers. According to Nancy Spain in her biography of Isabella Beeton, the immortal author of the archetypal cookery book, cutting patterns for dresses were invented by Isabella's publisher-husband Samuel Beeton, and appeared in his publication *The Englishwoman's Domestic Magazine*. But paper patterns had appeared many years before the Beetons came on the scene. Mrs Beeton does, however, describe a visit to Paris in search of suitable dresses, and must have visited Maison Worth, 'as we have seen several very tasty and elegant modes in EVENING DRESSES at a fashionable *maison des modes*.'

A star in the firmament of fashion

Young Mr Charles Frederick Worth started out as an apprentice draper at Swan & Edgar's in London. Worth senior, a solicitor, had a fondness for drink and gambling, and frittered away most of the family fortune, such as it was, so Charles had to find whatever work he could get. In 1838, Worth was apprenticed to the drapers in Piccadilly. It was hardly the path to fame and fortune or, if you prefer, rags to riches, though it was to prove so for Worth and, by the by, for another young draper who was born in 1866 during the height of Worth's career—the novelist H.G. Wells.

The appearance of the couturier on the growing fashion scene was bound to have occurred sooner or later, and in Paris. It was surely a matter of time before someone of Worth's calibre came along to direct single-handed the course of fashion history. Worth's achievement was due to quick-wittedness, a great deal of luck, and to being in the right place at the right time. He quit London for Paris and found employment in the respected establishment of Gagelin, silk mercers.

Over the following twelve years Worth developed a keen eye for the behaviour, characteristics, and above all the potential of textiles, especially of the silks of Lyon—satins, velvet and taffeta. And unlike most other draper's assistants with years of experience, Worth had flair and the sort of determination that founds dynasties. He was also living in a city where art was mostly encouraged and understood, where fashion ruled and

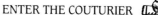

*A fashion plate of country
toilettes from Beeton's popular
Englishwoman's Domestic Magazine.
Mrs Beeton wrote fashion reports for
the magazine, and made regular trips
to Paris to buy the latest creations. In
this plate, the women are wearing
crinolines, the child full petticoats and
drawers under her linen dress. Mother
and child wear matching straw hats
and coiffures.*

where women of wealth and privilege from countries all over the
world focused their attention on matters of dress.

The transition from draper to dress designer came about
when Worth began designing dresses for his wife Marie, then a
model employed by Gagelin to show to advantage the shawls and
other accessories which the firm sold. Certain of Gagelin's
customers took a fancy to Marie Worth's dresses and requested
that Worth design for them too.

Supported by the customers' demands, he persuaded his
employers to open a dressmaking department, a move then
unprecedented, particularly in view of the fact that this would-be
designer/dressmaker was a man, and an Englishman at that!
Some thought the whole thing so ridiculous that they would have
nothing to do with it. Nevertheless, Worth's tenacity, diplomacy
and luck won for him some illustrious clients. The first of these
was the Princess Pauline Metternich, wife of the Austrian Ambassador to Paris, who described in her memoirs how Worth had
secured her patronage (and thereby his future reputation and
success) by offering to make her a gown for which she could name
her own price.

Said the Princess, 'There was to be a great ball at the
Tuileries—I wore the famous gown, and I can honestly say I have
rarely seen one so lovely nor better made. It was in white tulle

threaded with silver, sprinkled here and there with pink-centred daisies among wild grasses, which were veiled with white tulle. A white satin sash tied around the waist and I wore lots of diamonds. . . . Worth had his first success. The Empress immediately saw it was a *chef-d'oeuvre*. She came up to me at once and asked who had made this wonderfully pretty dress, so simple and yet so elegant. "An Englishman, madame, a new star that has risen in the firmament of fashion!" "And what is his name?" "Worth." "Very well," said the Empress, "the star must have some satellites, please instruct him to report to me tomorrow at ten o'clock!" Worth was launched and I was lost, for from that moment on dresses at 300 francs no longer saw the light of day.'

The House that Worth built

The Empress was Eugénie, wife of Napoleon III who, on his own admission was '*un parvenu dans la veritable acception du mot*'. His short-lived reign was marked by brilliant, and enduring, extravagance, an orgy of spending which included the restyling

The Princess Metternich, Worth's first influential client, photographed wearing a Worth dress in 1865. This was one of the 'flat-fronted' styles that would lead to Worth abolishing the crinoline altogether, in 1868, in favour of a back-fullness profile.

and rebuilding of Paris, and the establishment of a Court life that had echoes of Louis XIV and Versailles. For a royal Court it was both free-spending and free-thinking, its courtiers the upper echelons of industrial *nouveaux riches* who would look favourably on those who rose—like Worth—through the ranks.

By today's terms, the Court had more in common with show business than with the traditions of the *ancien régime*—history would never see the like again, nor would *haute couture*, under the guidance of Worth, be given such autonomy nor allowed such prodigality. With his sights set higher than Gagelin could accommodate, Worth quit and set up in partnership with a Swedish designer, Otto Bobergh, and together they founded the House of Worth & Bobergh in the Rue de la Paix. Maison Worth was granted a royal warrant, and in 1860 Worth became the imperial couturier.

The establishment was thus the first of the distinguished couture houses of Paris, wherein the design of women's dress, said Geoffrey Squire, became 'a true art, the conscious product of an individual mind which had elected to use the clothes of others as a medium for its own expression'. Fashionable dress 'began to be designed as an entity; conceived at the outset as providing the foundation for an ideal image.' So ideal, in fact, that being dressed by Worth was the only entrée to the world of high fashion in Paris.

The soil was eminently fertile, for such was the pace of fashion that huge sums of money were spent—some would say squandered—'for the pleasure of being smart'. When the chignon and false hair pieces were much in vogue during the 1860s, Paris as the major hair market of the world exported 300 tons to the United States, while 100 tons was retained for home use. England, meanwhile, was importing no less than 40,000 tons of iron, in addition to that produced at home, just for the manufacture of crinolines.

Against this background Worth was able to charge high prices for his *toilettes* or creations; a woman could compete with others in the quality, luxury and exclusivity of her costume and compete, too, on behalf of her husband—a man of substance showed his social and financial achievements by virtue of his wife's leisure and spending power. Worth could only have realized his singular accomplishment in the milieu of court society—international, competitive, and exceedingly wealthy. As such, it was a million miles away from the fashions of everyday life.

For a woman lower down the social scale, dresses could be bought, or ordered, from the newly established department stores, clothes that were made in-house by skilled, but unimaginative, dressmakers. Perhaps 'unimaginative' is unfair—creativity was the prerogative of those who could afford it, and dressmakers were not hired to be imaginative. They were hired to sew for at least twelve hours a day, and in 1861 there were 286,000 of them in England and Wales, singing the song of the shirt.

This was dressmaking, but the staff of 1200 at Maison Worth were dress designing—virtually a new profession. A dress would be designed specifically to suit one lady, according to her figure, her colour, her deportment, her personality—and Worth's own ideals. Of prime importance was the fit. A robe by Worth was

All self-respecting ladies of fashion would have a selection of tea gowns in their wardrobes for informal occasions, though this tea gown by Worth is hardly informal. It has a high, lace collar, a draped caftan of Watteau pleats, and a waisted dress—probably à la princess—with stamped maroon velvet floral designs on a beige ground.

Masquerade balls and parties gave the Court of the Second Empire a further excuse for extravagant dressing, and encouraged designers to excel themselves in fantasy. The peacock dress was created by Worth for the Princess de Sagan in 1864 to be worn at the Bal des Bêtes. *The train was covered in peacock plumes, and the head-dress fashioned in feathers to the shape of a miniature bird. Peacock dresses became a speciality of the house.*

so perfect in every stitch and seam that it required only one fitting, and in this he was a perfectionist. He had the pick of the finest materials available, and in particular silks from the *soieries* of Lyon from whom Worth ordered exclusive designs.

Five gowns for tea and never worn twice . . .

From his relatively humble beginnings in a small Lincolnshire village, Charles Frederick Worth had become the impresario who was given a free hand to stage manage the most glittering social extravaganza in modern history. In many respects it was all Worth's fault anyway—he had raised the art of dress to such a degree that *haute couture* was now taken for granted. The Empress's new clothes were worn only once for an official occasion, and this had a 'knock on' effect since Court ladies (also dressed by Worth) were expected to follow the royal example. Due to the increased frequency of state occasions in the Second Empire, the palace servants and the theatres, who by tradition inherited the cast-offs, were literally swamped in tulle and brocade creations, all by Worth.

The imperial couturier had to maintain the exceptional standards that he himself had set and produce dresses in variety and number for these state functions. There were, for instance, four balls every season attended by over two thousand lady guests, most of whom demanded to be dressed by Worth. There

A grand reception at the Palais des Tuileries in 1867, four years before the end of the Second Empire, the Siege of Paris, and the Franco-Prussian War. In T. van Elven's painting, the Empress Eugénie is accompanied by Czar Alexander II, and the two future adversaries—Napoleon III and the King of Prussia. The Empress is wearing a Worth dress, and so, probably, were all the other ladies present at the occasion.

Evening toilette *with Worth's new fan train, from* Harper's Bazaar, *1873. The dress is in black Chambery gauze with gold stripes over black silk. The bustle was most pronounced at this time.*

were additional parties, receptions for visiting royalty, and out-of-town excursions. Guests invited to the imperial chateaux at Fontainebleau and Compiègne were obliged to take trunks full of dresses, none of which could be worn twice, as etiquette decreed.

The American Mrs Charles Moulton took eleven trunks containing 'eight day costumes (counting my travelling suit), the green cloth dress for the hunt, which I was told was absolutely necessary, seven ball dresses, five gowns for tea.' Mrs Moulton's gowns would have to be unique, and in no way similar to those worn by other guests—also dressed by Worth—except in their being the style of the period. Worth, as always, met the challenge and retained the confidence of his clients. 'Women who come to me want to ask for my ideas, not to follow out their own,' he told the journalist Adolphus. 'They deliver themselves to me in confidence, and I decide for them; that makes them happy. If I tell them they are suited, they need no further evidence. My signature on their gown suffices!'

A fashionable lady in nineteenth-century Paris spent most of her time changing from one dress to another according to the occasion or time of day. There were day dresses, or *toilettes de ville*—even *grandes toilettes de ville*. There were *toilettes de campagne* which Worth revolutionized by raising hems so that

they no longer trailed in the mud. There were evening dresses or *toilettes de soirée* and *de diner*, and the lavish *toilettes de bal*.

  Ball gowns and evening gowns were always worn with shoulders bare, and usually with bare arms, while day dresses left only the face and hands uncovered, so that when gloves and bonnets were worn there wasn't much bare flesh to be seen. Some of Worth's *toilettes* survive in the costume museums, especially in America, but there are surprisingly few when you consider the vast number the couturier must have turned out during the Second Empire, when the candles were burning day and night in his workshops.

The discipline of fashion — Ton is now chic

There is an evening dress from Worth & Bobergh in the Victoria and Albert Museum, London, in pale silk satin, trimmed with beads and machine embroidery and machine-made lace, lined with white silk, and with a boned bodice. It has much in common with the sack dresses of the mid eighteenth century, to which couturiers frequently turned for inspiration, as they did with the *polonaise* style in the 1870s. Worth's evening dress has a train, a feature shared with ball gowns and court costume—the rending of silk fabric from a misplaced foot must have been a familiar sound

Visiting costume, also from Harper's Bazaar, *1875, designed in the Princess style—the corsage and tablier skirt are shaped without a waist seam. The dress is of strawberry satin with bands of black velvet. The back-fullness has been slimmed down, and within a year will have gone altogether.*

Worth's dedicated skill as a dressmaker, and his continuous search for simplicity combined with elegance of cut and line, led to the development of the Princess style—ABOVE and RIGHT. It was to become a basic technique that other couturiers would adopt for their own designs.

in nineteenth century Society. The dress also has what Worth terms the 'Princess line' where the bodice joins the skirt in one piece, without a waist seam, the fitting achieved by using long darts from the bust to the hips, and named after the charming and popular Alexandra of Wales, who became a Worth client.

Worth's aim was always one of simplicity, even though he was working during a period of ornate fabrics and trimmings. His eye for harmony through contrast can be seen in a day dress of 1887–89, also in the Victoria and Albert Museum, with a bodice and sleeves in dark green wool and a skirt of strawberry-coloured figured satin, the green wool descending in long panels each rounded at the ends and alternating with the silk. It is striking yet restrained, for Worth disciplined fashion, as Brummell had done, replacing Brummell's ton with chic—a word he perhaps invented —and always with a pure and elegant line. Charles Dickens, himself an aspiring dandy, said of Worth's designs that they had a 'touch of genius, for there is as much talent in knowing what to abate as in knowing what to add.'

For the remainder of his career, Worth designed for the royal courts of Europe and the Court at St Petersburg. Only Queen Victoria eluded Worth's tape and scissors, perhaps because she was in permanent mourning after Albert's death in 1861 (although Worth designed mourning dress) but probably because, as his biographer Diana de Marly suggests, she could not countenance the idea of a male dressmaker or, as the press called Worth, a 'man-milliner'. It simply wasn't the done thing . . .

But Worth was practically a Frenchman, and became widely influential and exceedingly wealthy. Only Balenciaga, in our times, would surpass Worth as a superb tailor and inventive designer, but on a more modest scale of production. Maison Worth almost collapsed during the Siege of Paris and the decline and fall of the Second Empire, having lived through a fairy tale beyond recall. That the House survived is partly due to Worth's having found the time to establish a dynasty: his sons Gaston and Jean-Philippe became couturiers, as did his grandsons Jean-Charles and Jacques, and great-grandsons Roger and Maurice.

The most evocative memory of that past age came from Jean-Philippe, as described by Edith Saunders in *The Age of Worth*: 'The young Jean Worth watched the Empress skating one day, and a picture was fixed in his mind which did not fade with the years. She was with the Princess Metternich and two other ladies of high rank. As they glided smoothly in a row, they held out before them in their eight neatly gloved hands a rod covered in velvet. They were wearing extremely short crinolines, so short that they barely covered their knees and billowed up higher in the breeze. Beneath were wide velvet knickers, fastened under the knees. Their legs were gaitered, and their flashing silver skates were strapped to high-heeled, pointed boots. They wore short jackets, drawn in tightly at the waist and trimmed with sable and chinchilla, and small velvet toques were perched on the front of their heads.' It takes a budding couturier to remember dress details like that, and Jean-Philippe was to maintain the reputation of Maison Worth.

*T*he latter part of the nineteenth century was dominated by the rise and fall—and decisive comeback—of the bustle. The demise of the crinoline, and emergence of the bustle, is attributed to Worth, but it effectively coincides with the Young cycle, since the back-fullness profile was overdue and its reappearance imminent. Young thought that designers were swayed by and subject to the great fashion cycles, and that their pre-eminence depended to a certain extent on the gift of prescience —the ability to see which way trends were going.

Whether the question 'did the crinoline fall or was it pushed?' is valid or not, the fact seems to be that Worth was the catalyst. In 1868 he discarded the crinoline, and the bustle made a somewhat abrupt appearance. A collapsible contraption like a mouse's cage supported the bustle and the large, fan-like train that rode over it. This was in 1873. Two years later Worth had slimmed down the line, reducing the back-fullness but retaining the train, and by 1876 the bustle, after only eight years, had gone.

The 1860s was the decade of the chignon, and braided false hair pieces or falling curls were de rigueur. *Bonnets were generally rather simple affairs, decorated with a single feather, a plume or a few flowers.*

In place of the bustle came the cuirasse bodice, in which the firm, boned bodice of the day dress now descended in a smooth line over the hips, down the front (a corset with a spoon-busk was required to maintain the upright shape of the torso) and continued with a close-fitting skirt to the knees. This made bending forward difficult, not to mention the gentle art of sitting down. Furthermore the train, and the abundance of material inherited from the crinoline days, meant that women hobbled along dragging a riot of drapery with pleated flounces and ruching and cascades of ribbons.

Not everyone was quite so encumbered, and although Worth's designs were such that they brought harmony to disorder, his patterns were pirated on a huge scale and freely interpreted. There were also those who observed the dictates of the Rational Dress Society, which eschewed boned bodices and tight sleeves and generally opted for free-style dressing. There were simple town dresses, too, based on the Princess style, and with a modest train or none at all. Most women, however, appeared in public as though they had wrapped themselves in a theatre curtain and were struggling to get out. It was an unbecoming style, but the one that followed was hardly an improvement—the return of the bustle.

It would appear that the interference with the gradual transition that should have taken place from the bell cycle to the back-fullness cycle was premature. 'Any attempt by the fashion trades,' warned Young, 'to alter the fundamental cycle type before the time for change has arrived, will meet with failure.' In 1881 the bustle returned, this time it was narrower, but became exaggeratedly angular, like a shelf. With the bustle, women carried large fans, or parasols, and there was a fashion for elaborate fan-shaped hair combs or coronets.

When men discarded the fancy waistcoat in favour of one which matched the suit, women adopted it for their own wear. A variation of the *polonaise* style, now exactly a century old, made a brief reappearance as it had on the first bustle dresses of 1870. The bustle, sometimes called the tournure, was supported on a wire cage or a device of fluted rows, one above the other, of stiffened calico, whalebones and horsehair. Contemporary writers complained that the style had reached absurd proportions, although they also feared the return of the crinoline. But the back-fullness was gradually slimming down, heralding the return of the tubular cycle and a new century.

Yellow wool and scarlet corsets

The theory of *zeitgeist*—the spirit of the age—seems somewhat defeated by the extraordinary fashions of the 1880s, when the excessive material made dresses appear to defy the concept of freedom for women and the great stirrings of emancipation. Men, by contrast, were dressed in matching coat and waistcoat, though trousers might be of a different and lighter material. The middle class man now had the wealth and leisure to follow such sports as golf, walking, Lakeland climbing and continental mountaineering, cycling and shooting. The tweed industry were happy to oblige by designing and manufacturing Norfolk jackets, matching suits of

In the 1880s, during the craze for cycling, magazines attempted to introduce a 'decent' cycling dress for women. The long, divided skirt was weighted at the hem with lead, to conceal the ankles. Said James Laver, 'Some of the divided skirts were a grotesque attempt to combine the outline of contemporary dress with the comfort of bloomers.' Bloomers, also called 'Turkish trousers', were a more successful revival of Amelia Bloomer's invention and met with approval—more or less—from Victorian society.

jacket, waistcoat and knickerbockers with boots and gaiters, and tweed caps. By mid century white flannels came in for cricket and boating. Overcoats were much in vogue: the double-breasted Wellesley; the single-breasted Palmerston, with its big collar and lapels; the long Chesterfield with high-buttoned lapels of velvet or fur; the Gladstone edged with astrakhan; the big Ulster overcoat with a short cape around the shoulders, or the Inverness with a cape down to the waist. The top hat, popular headwear for over a century, was still in use, and underneath the suit men had taken to woollen combinations.

Made of yellowish wool and close fitting to the body, woollen 'combs' could be itchy, but they kept one warm, especially those converted to the new crusade, led by Dr Gustave Jaeger with

Caps, blazers, and 'long shorts' were favoured by university sportsmen. In 1885 this group of gentlemen scholars from the Cambridge Boat Race crew posed for their photograph, taken by the firm of Hills Saunders. The picture must have been shot before the event, judging by the group's demeanour, for in that year the Boat Race was won by Oxford . . .

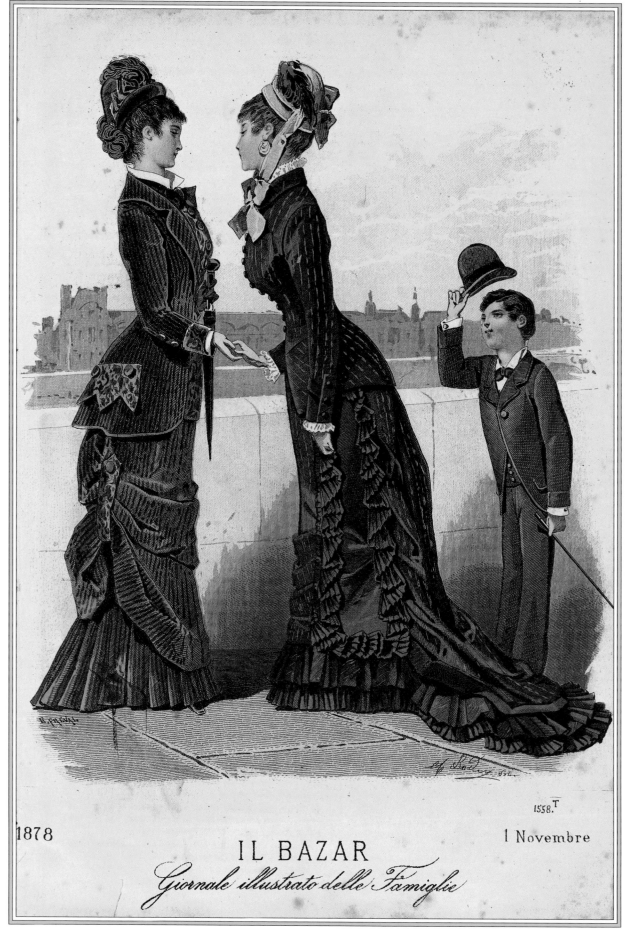

1878

IL BAZAR
Giornale illustrato delle Famiglie

1 Novembre

1558.^T

his doctrine of Sanitary Woollen Clothing (comparable to our current preoccupation with wholefoods and dieting). Jaeger's premise—that 'wool is meant by nature to protect animal life; and, instead of preventing it, it assists the evaporation of the emanations coming from the body. It is therefore warm in winter, cool in summer, healthy at all times'—was given the support of the Rational Dress Society. Dr Jaeger, the earnest German author of *Health Culture*, was not the first to promote woollen underwear, but his professional status, combined with the vogue—if that's the right word—for dress reform, served to inspire a happy brotherhood known as the 'Woollenites'.

The movement encouraged the ever-present eccentric side of the English character with its occasional impulse to proselytize, without touching on the need to ridicule. Anyway, it was more than sufficient to found the Jaeger Company, and to launch Britain's own undyed woollen garment industry in addition. So the Woollenites, men and women alike, faced a bright future hand in hand, wearing their undyed combinations. Yet the Woollen Movement was no flash in the pan, remaining vigorous for over thirty years until the lightweight cotton/wool mixture for underclothes was introduced.

Against this somewhat whimsical, woolly background, several discoveries were being made which would have far-reaching effects on the world of fashion. One of these was the invention of rayon, or artificial silk, the first of the man-made fibres, by Comte Hilaire de Chardonnet. The dye industry had already been revitalized by the discovery, by William Perkin (while experimenting in his garden shed) of aniline, and the dye alazarin by Heinrich Caro in Germany. The late Victorians were thus dazed by a rash of brightly coloured dresses—not to mention scarlet corsets and violet knickers—brought about by science wedded to fashion.

Towards the end of the century domestic inventions came thick and fast: in 1880 the gas fire; in 1882 H.W. Seeley invented the electric iron. Then came the carpet-sweeper and the telephone (to enable one to call one's couturier), and the drapery stores were mechanized by the adding machine and the cash-register. The fashionable could dance to the phonograph, wearing clothes produced by fabrics made on the new automatic loom. The same clothes, delicately coloured with a blush of alazarin, could now be photographed in colour by the autochrome process. The Age of Realism was realized by photography, a medium that was to have a profound influence on the fashions of the twentieth century—it was all there in colour and sturdy black and white.

While Degas painted his realist studies of yawning laundresses and weary milliners, Nadar, the 'Titian of Photography,' sat Manet, Corot, Dumas, Baudelaire, Berlioz and Wagner in front of his camera—warts and all. In England Julia Margaret Cameron shot pictures of Darwin, Tennyson and Carlyle.

The fashions of the 1880s seemed to be holding back this inexorable progress of inventive endeavour. They were, in brief, matronly and conservative, as feudal and restrictive as the fashions of Louis XIV—the last gesture of a courtly age. The ladies wearing the bustle of the 1880s passed like a ship of the line into

The ideal of a slender, natural body shape came into fashion in the mid 1870s, and was maintained by the aid of the stoutly-boned, long-waisted cuirasse bodice, which slimmed down the hips and reduced the back-fullness. The line of the skirt then descended to a demi-train or flowing train. The figure on the left has an overskirt caught up at the sides à la polonaise, *as it was called, though rather different from the true* polonaise *of the late eighteenth century.*

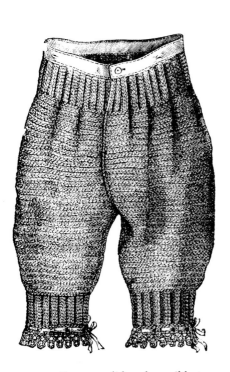

Secure, solid and sensible—Victorian knitted drawers.

history. For a brief moment in 1800 fashion had been freed by the simple attire of the neoclassic *mode à la grecque*, but it retired abashed before the overtly feminine modes of the 1830s, expanded into the stately crinolines of the 1860s, and took refuge, finally, in the bustle.

Shock and horror—The darker side of fashion

The way ahead was already established. Women wearing Amelia Bloomer's bloomers cycled into the future, singing 'Daisy, Daisy'. In Paris *La Belle Epoque* was kicking up its heels, and Toulouse Lautrec was formulating a style that would be picked up by William Nicholson (The Beggerstaff Brothers), embellished by Aubrey Beardsley, used by Charles Rennie Mackintosh in designing the Glasgow Tea Rooms, and realized in fashion by Paul Poiret and the fashion artist George Lepape, a style that culminated in a curious hybrid of Celtic/Japanese—Art Nouveau.

Before all this could take place in chronological sequence, fashions underwent the metamorphosis from the bustle and back-fullness profile to the gored, flared skirt of the 1890s, with the huge gigot sleeves, the impossibly tiny waist, and the hat, decorated with hummingbirds, that had more to do with the taxidermist than the milliner.

Out of this confusion came the Gibson Girl, created by Charles Dana Gibson in one of his masterly pen drawings. This 'Big American Girl' was determinedly self-assured, part college girl, part fashionable beauty, her hat perched jauntily on her pompadoured head, followed everywhere by male admirers. This new American girl was not just exceptionally pretty, she could look you straight in the eye, had a firm handshake, and strode from the nineteenth into the twentieth century emancipated, confident and chic.

The image of the Gibson Girl gave women encouragement to cope with the difficulties of *fin de siècle* reality: 'She wore a wide-brimmed hat that caught the breezes, a high choking collar of satin or linen, and a flaring gored skirt that swept the street on all sides. Her full-sleeved shirtwaist had cuffs that were eternally getting dirty, her stock was always crushed and rumpled at the end of the day, and her skirt was a bitter trial. Its heavy brush binding had to be replaced every few weeks, for constant contact with the pavement reduced it to a dirty fringe in no time at all. In wet weather the full skirt got soaked and icy. Even in fair weather its wearer had to bunch it in great folds and devote one hand to nothing else but the carrying of it.'

If this was the darker side of fashion, there was help at hand. The 1890s clung to the old values, but the twentieth century was to revolutionize fashions. Although there were other couturiers—Henry Creed, John Redfern, Mme Paquin, Doeuillet and Doucet—the nineteenth century belongs to Charles Frederick Worth, who died in 1895. Within the decade the iron rule of the corset would be shattered, and replaced by a simple girdle. The waistline would go, and women would be liberated. The tubular cycle would begin with elegant, shealth-like dresses that recalled the old Empire line, dresses that would be slit down the side to reveal—shock and horror—calves and ankles!

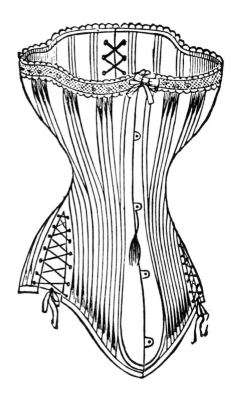

Specialist corset designers and manufacturers enjoyed a boom following the demise of the crinoline and the introduction of the bustle and cuirasse bodice. Corsets had to fit tightly over the hips and down the front. More rigid corsets were designed, with finely engineered boning, intricately-shaped gussets, elastic insertions, and the spoon-shaped busk of steel.

The couturier responsible for this outrage, which would shock even a Gibson Girl, declared, 'It was in the name of Liberty that I brought about my first revolution, by deliberately laying siege to the corset.' The couturier was Paul Poiret, 'the evil genius of high fashion'. His designs were to have much the same effect as the Impressionists and Cubists were having on the art establishment. Fashion, as the previous centuries understood it, would never be the same again.

The bustle returned in the 1880s and with it many-layered, weighty toilettes, featuring the draped folds, lavishly trimmed. Jackets, meticulously tailored and with a flaring peplum, helped accentuate the bustle. Hats, laden with feathers, threatened to take flight.

LN 934

LEFT The huge, ballooning gigot or leg-of-mutton sleeves of the mid-1890s gave width to the shoulders and so emphasized the narrow waist. Additional emphasis is provided here by the crossover lapels, echoed by the design of the skirt. Gigot sleeves were a short-lived mode (last seen in the 1820s).

RIGHT Charles Dana Gibson's immortal Gibson Girl was a wholly American creation with her shirt-waist, plain skirt and pompadour coiffure. She was the image of the New Woman. Gibson had based his girl on the three Langhorne sisters, one of whom became Lady Astor, while another became Mrs Gibson . . .

Chapter 6

LINGERIE AND ANARCHY

1900-1914

The corset reached the peak of its development in the Edwardian period, when the S-bend design forced female torsos into the curves of a swan's neck. Most women accepted it without complaint, feeling that fashion must be obeyed: only a leader of fashion could hope to effect a change. While women's underwear became more rigid, the underwear of the Edwardian male was a simple vest and long-john pants, or the one-piece 'combination' known in America as the 'union suit'.

If lingerie can provoke its own revolutions, there were several activists around to bring about the demise of the corset. One such person was heiress Caresse Crosby, who invented the brassière, another was that 'designer of dishcloths', Paul Poiret. He, and the couturier Madeleine Vionnet, both claim to have liberated women from the whalebone embrace of the S-bend. Women could now breath, but they couldn't walk when Poiret introduced his notorious sheath-like skirt, the 'hobble'. As if this wasn't enough, women hid themselves beneath enormous hats, burdened down with fruit and feathers. The hat and the hobble were the last of the rigid fashions; World War I and the emancipation of women ended their sway.

*T*he Gibson Girl marked a progress in social attitudes towards women, and so did the typewriter. At the turn of the century there were five million working women in America, birthplace of the revolutionary Remington, 100,000 earning a living as typists. Britain's 1901 census does not even list typing as an occupation, and it isn't until 1911 that we discover the existence of 980 typists; just ten years later there were 420,000! As for France, the typewriter was displayed as a mere curiosity at the Paris World Fair. Thirty-seven per cent of French women went out to work, but should they covet the life-style of their American counterparts, the French establishment press reminded them that, 'A woman's standing in modern society depends entirely on the man she marries or works for.'

So much for liberty and equality, though the popular women's journal *La Mode Illustrée* helped women to be chic without being independent, advising readers on how to remodel old dresses, and to avoid what they called 'operatic' fashions (the adornments of *haute couture*) in the pursuit of good taste and embourgeoisement, or 'upwards mobility'. To a limited extent, French women were conscious of American styles and fashions, and very admiring of American household appliances, and, although few French women had the opportunity to visit the United States, Americans flocked to Paris.

Such was the attraction of *La Belle Epoque*, the fabled decade before the turn of the century when Paris was uninhibitedly gay, that American Express opened its Paris office in 1895, and the couture houses were sustained largely by American clients—only 37 per cent of clients were French. From the trunk-loads of dresses bought at Worth, Paquin, Redfern, Doucet and Callot Soeurs, and shipped to America, copies were made for the mass market, and the mass market for these clothes consisted, by and large, of comfortably-off married women who kept the home fires burning.

By 1905 the young American typist—mainly unmarried—had evolved a new all-American fashion—the shirtwaist blouse worn with a skirt, bought from department stores such as Sears Roebuck, whose now legendary catalogue offered 150 different versions of the shirtwaist style, secured by a petersham belt. Yet even the Gibson Girl was restricted by her corset, her gigot sleeves and her long skirt. Furthermore, fashion dictated that she wore a hat. She might get away with a simple straw boater, but for most women, this was the age of the hat, as well as being the last gasp of the restrictive corset.

Coquetry with discomfort—The ultimate corset

The corset was still the anchor of feminine fashions and the subject of regular and passionate debate among those who advocated Rational Dress, the medical profession who warned against tight lacing, and those who pursued the dream of the perfect figure. Such was Mrs Eric Pritchard, who in her book *The Cult of Chiffon*, advised readers to go to a first-class corsetière. 'No woman should be with less than three pairs of corsets in wear at once, all of the same make. The woman who wears exactly the wrong corset is almost as hopeless as she who wears none at all.'

The blouse, finely detailed and elaborate in contrast to the plain skirt, was the most notable feature of fashions of La Belle Epoque *and Edwardian era. They were mostly of Japanese silk and crêpe de Chine, trimmed and inset with Valenciennes lace and machine embroidery. Every woman had a blouse for day and evening wear. For the less well-off they were an expensive item, so that home-dressmaking patterns for 'Dainty Blouses' of Jap silk, muslin and lace were a weekly feature in* Home Notes *magazine.*

Supplément au N°
du 15 Juin 1906

Reproduction interdite

Imp. Falconer, Paris.

N°. 5382

'JOURNAL DES DEMOISELLES

Modes de Paris

52, Rue St Georges.

Parfumerie HOUBIGANT 19, Faub.º St Honoré

Corset advertisements, carefully retouched, showed the achievement of the ideal figure with a wasp-waist, rounded hips, ample bust, and provocative frills and bows. If these failed to create a stampede to the stores, there was inspiration and confirmation in the curvaceous figures of such celebrated beauties as Camille Clifford, Britain's response to the Gibson Girl; the French actress Réjane, and the soprano Mary Garden of the Opéra Comique; even the redoubable and 'divine' Sarah Bernhardt, had her following among the more mature ladies, for whom the importance of being corseted was never questioned.

The wasp-waist had become the prerequisite of the bell-shaped and back-fullness profiles that had dominated styles for seventy years, and corsetières overreached themselves in tailoring ingenuity, their artistry culminating in the infamous 'S' curve corset of 1904–5. This had a low bust, with a heavy and straight busk down the front, the sides arching high over the hips. The design forced the bust up and forward, while the inflexible abdominal busk forced hips, thighs and bottom rearwards. A lightweight 'negligee' corset for the boudoir seems to have been the only alternative, and it must have been this item that Mrs Pritchard refers to when she says, 'The corset today at its best is quite the most hygienic and beautiful little garment yet produced, chiefly, perhaps, because there is hardly anything of it.'

Any erotic message stimulated by the 'S' curve corset was neither deliberate nor subconscious, but incidental, although it did emphasize on the so-called 'erogenous zones' of sexual interest. The corset and the curves it produced were the final stages of a style that was about to be succeeded by another—back-fullness making way for the tubular profile. The lingerie that accompanied the corset was by now a department of fashion in its own right. In 1901 the first trade journal devoted to corsetry, *Les Dessous Elégants*, was published, and Mrs Pritchard advised the wise woman with a limited dress allowance to invest a great deal of it in underwear.

Lingerie became one more aspect of fashion that could be exploited by manufacturers and journalists, and became indispensible to the fashionable lady. Edwardian women took the subject seriously combining coquetry with comfort, so that silk or satin knickers, worn with country clothes, had detachable linings of flannel, linen or washing silk to make one 'warm and cosy'. Lingerie would further be embroidered or finished with lace trimmings.

Silk stockings, hidden beneath long skirts, and therefore viewed only by those intimately privileged, might be embroidered with fetching designs—snakes were popular, entwined around the legs. Even in those heady days of liberated lingerie, propriety ruled, so that the lingerie counter of a department store was always upstairs. This, Alison Adburgham informs us, in *Shops and Shopping*, was so that 'there was no possible danger of a man walking through the department. Hosiery, however, was always on the ground floor; and this was not without its subtle suggestiveness. The elaborate frill of an underskirt was the only thing a gentleman could hope to observe occasionally—there was also the glimpse of an ankle.'

A cover illustration from La Nouvelle Mode, *1901. A* toilette de visites *with a pèkiné (candy striped) bolero, the plush revers matching the cashmere blouse. The bolero jacket was very smart—the glimpse of an ankle very provocative.*

Dainty lingerie from The Queen *magazine. A nightdress in 1900 was as elaborate as a blouse, with its high collar and frou-frou of embroidered cambric and lace trimmings.*

Underwear began to take on a special significance when the decorative elements began to reveal a deliberate emphasis. This is an important aspect of all women's clothes, and the reason for fashion's infinite variations on a basic theme. The gratuitous display of purely non-functional enrichment is fundamentally erotic. Manufacturers were quick to see the huge potential of the lingerie market. Thus, Edwardian lingerie achieved a high degree of frou-frou with lace, broderie anglaise, silk, satin, mercerized cotton, cashmere, merino, cambric, and crêpe de Chine. The men were restricted to wool combinations and flannel vests and drawers. What they lacked in variety they made up for in stripes and colour: pink, lavender, light blue and red were worn, and white was reserved for Sundays, since the paterfamilias was duty-bound to set an example of cleanliness in mind, spirit, body and underwear on the Sabbath.

Plain or coloured, men's underwear was stoutly anti-erotic and purely functional: America's version of the all-in-one vest and pants—the union suit for instance—had a buttoned flap at the rear and buttons to the front, and was made of cotton, silk or wool. For winter wear, designers employed the merino wool-cotton mixture, patented under the name of 'Viyella' in 1894 by the British hosiery firm of William Hollins. As men's 'combs' were utilitarian, there was little room for improvement. But in the early part of the century, the American Cooper Underwear Company introduced the Kenosha Klosed Krotch one-piece garment. Here, two pieces of the body fabric lapped over each other like an X, but could be drawn apart when the occasion demanded. On such modest inventions does the future of great nations depend . . .

When an Edwardian couple retired for the night, she would wear a nightdress while he might now have switched to the new vogue for pyjamas which superseded the flannel nightgown and conical hat of the previous century. In the morning, his trousers would be taken from the recently invented press that produced a sharp crease front and back. He still had to struggle into a shirt that, inconveniently, couldn't be unbuttoned all the way down, but it might have modest stripes of blue or pink, and even a turn-down white collar.

Boaters and bowlers—Hats for all occasions

The young Edwardian man, clean-shaven and raring to go (by car if he could afford it), might wear a double-breasted jacket with his creased trousers, the lapels buttoned high on the chest, with either a bow-tie or a 'four-in-hand' (the narrow straight tie worn today) and, of course, a hat. Everyone wore a hat. Men could wear a variety of types, but etiquette dictated how and when, and nobody, regardless of class and status, went out bareheaded. An English gentleman always wore his hat perfectly straight on his head. To wear one's 'topper' at an angle marked one out as an unutterable cad. The straw hat—called a 'boater' in England since it was favoured by the boating fraternity—was worn by all classes and by several nations, especially the French and Americans, enhancing the personal charm of Maurice Chevalier, and the clowning of Harold Lloyd, in the 1920s. Tweed caps with a peak were worn by the Edwardian working-class man, and by the

SOME ATTRACTIVE SPRING HATS

1. PALE LAVENDER FANCY STRAW BRAID, LAVENDER VELVET AND PLUME. 2. WHITE ROSES, FORGET-ME-NOTS, BLUE RIBBON. 3. ÉCRU STRAW, BUTTON, BRAID, WHITE PLUMES. 4. WHITE HORSEHAIR STRAW, YELLOW DAISIES AND BLACK VELVET RIBBON. 5. WHITE SILK MULL AND LACE, WHITE BIRDS. 6. PALE BLUE STRAW, PINK BUDS, FORGET-ME-NOTS, BLACK VELVET RIBBON. 7. BLACK AND WHITE STRAW, WHITE SILK, COQ FEATHER BREAST. 8. ÉCRU STRAW, BROWN STRAW BRAID, BROWN WINGS.

upper-class man, though there was a difference in style and a gentleman would only wear a tweed cap in the country. In town he would be seen with a top hat, black and glossy, at Ascot with a grey topper, and in the City wearing a bowler.

The suggested origin of the name 'bowler' are varied and mostly unconvincing, but it was probably so called because of its inverted, bowl-like shape. Some versions, such as the tall 'billy-cock' were worn by street traders; in America the bowler, the boater and the tweed cap were constrained neither by hierarchy nor geography but were worn by everyone everywhere, the bowler being popularized as the 'Derby' and worn in black, brown or grey. In England, Edward VII started the fashion for grey bowlers, as he did the Homburg which he brought back as a souvenir from Bad Homburg in Prussia—a grey, felt hat with a wide brim and a dent along the crown. Explorers, artists, film pioneers, and gentry visiting the Riviera sported the straw Panama hat, and the new breed of motorist had the leather cap with ear flaps and big goggles, later adopted by aviators.

Men's unchanging styles could only reflect fashions in minor accents, and in foibles of dress, or by imitating the styles of a higher social strata. That excellent fashion writer and *Times* journalist, the late Prudence Glynn, wrote of Edward VII and Bismarck, that 'from their sleek macassar'd heads through their grave beards to their neat pointed boots they were the images on which millions of men from vastly different surroundings cast themselves for their leisure moments. Miners changed into suits for their Sunday best, and when the Prince of Wales left one waistcoat button undone, either through negligence or flatulence, it was an occasion for a fashion note.' It was probably also a gesture of relaxed informality. Penelope Byrde, in her book *The Male Image* says that the habit dates at least from 1820, and even before that the waistcoats of the eighteenth century had sham buttonholes with buttons left unfastened.

The symbol of the unfastened button became a mark of élitism among the Battle of Britain pilots in World War II, when the top button of the uniform was left undone. Symbolism in dress is a specialized field of study, but many people have drawn attention to the probable phallic symbolism of the top hat and certain military helmets. Similarly, women's hats, and especially those of the early 1900s with their abundance of fur and feather, fruit and flowers, may be seen to represent the female principle.

Women's hats of the first Edwardian decade were very large and out of proportion to the sheath-like dress with its flared hem and generous pleats. There is no ulterior sexual significance here, though. The hats were large to compensate for the relatively sudden loss of bulk below. Anyway, hats have always been a wonderfully versatile and decorative element of women's fashions, and they too have their recurring cycles of shape and size.

Unfortunately, they also used, and brought about the decline of, some rare species of birds. Commented *The Lady's World*, 'One could have collected from the persons of fine ladies a whole aviary of birds and nests complete with eggs, beetles, cock-chafers, centipedes, lizards and scorpions, rats, mice, snakes,

The tubular, linear style was well established by the turn of the century, assisted by longer corsets, dresses with flowing lines—as in this pleated toilette de campagne—*and accentuated by high collars. The collar could be replaced for evening wear—if you could afford it—with a choker of pearls, a fashion introduced to English society by Queen Alexandra, who could afford it.*

The topper, the bowler or Derby, the Homburg, and the boater. In the Victorian and Edwardian periods there was a hat for every occasion, and everyone wore a hat.

105

spiders and flies, together with skins of various beasts of prey.' In the service of millinery some 200 million birds were slaughtered each year. The luckless egret was almost wiped out, as were many brilliantly plumed hummingbirds, whose secure presence on the heads of fashionable Edwardian ladies owed as much to the taxidermist as to the hatter. Both trades used mercury salts as preservatives (the hatters mercuric nitrate and the taxidermists mercuric chloride), poisonous chemicals that were said to induce, among other symptoms, St Vitus's Dance or convulsions, hence the saying, 'mad as a hatter'—but not 'mad as a taxidermist'.

The hats may have been fashionable, but they were not chic. They were, according to Gwen Raverat, 'enormous, over-trimmed hats, which were fixed to the armature of one's puffed-out hair by long and murderous pins. On the top of an open bus, in a wind, their mighty sails flapped agonizingly at their anchorage, and pulled out one's hair by the handful.'

Add this to the attire of the lady described at the end of Chapter 5, whose skirt was a bitter trial, and who had to bunch it in great folds in order to carry it along with her, and you begin to see how the passion for fashion is not a flame easily quenched, even in women with modest means. It is the special preserve, the domain and *raison d'être*, of many women, their strength and their unity. Few men can understand, and less appreciate, the female response to matters of fashion. It is not a frivolous, but a serious business, and like all successful businesses, fashion needs direction, formulation, inspiration and a potential market.

This is not the same thing as the captive audience enjoyed by Louis XIV at the Court of Versailles, but a modern, vigorous and dynamic market that can be swayed by a visionary in league with artists and textile manufacturers quick enough to tune into current moods and fancies. Such a visionary was Paul Poiret.

An American advertisement for 'Conformo Corsets', a straight-fronted design for the slender, long-hipped styles of 1908, but the full bust was still fashionable.

*F*ashion needs couturiers, even couturiers like Poiret —arrogant, extravagant, wilful, and ultimately self-destructive; Poiret went from riches to rags and died in poverty, but while he was active as a couturier, no star shone more brightly in the fashion firmament previously dominated by Worth and noted by the Princess Metternich. Poiret was the first couturier—and he has had many imitators—to sacrifice style and tradition for sensation in the service of art, the art of dress design being to him part of the visual, plastic arts. His clothes were sensational because they were fashion in the abstract and decidedly *avant-garde*, since Poiret was in regular contact with and was influenced by the art and artists of his time. Whereas Charles Frederick Worth's influences stemmed from the world of academic art, Poiret was 'modern' in that he designed during a period of artistic anarchy—at least in the opinion of the public.

The turn of the century saw the reluctant acceptance of Impressionism—indeed, it was the heyday of 'isms', or seemingly subversive art movements such as the Japanese-influenced Nabis (via Gaugin), Art Nouveau (from William Morris, Whistler, Beardsley, the Pre-Raphaelites), the Cubists, Fauves and Expressionists. These movements inspired the illustrators—always more

closely in touch with popular art styles—and the fashion artists, Lepape, Benito, Mucha, Drian and Marty. Poiret's association with the *avant-garde* was not in the tradition of couture. Even though couture was a mere fifty years old, it was traditionally based on the patronage of high society, wealth and privilege; Poiret needed such patronage, but he would bite the hand that fed him.

Poiret's ideals were not in accord with the opulent and luxurious fashions that the leading couturiers, such as Mme Paquin and Jean-Philippe Worth produced. Worth thought Poiret's ideas were 'vulgar' and his dresses 'mere dishcloths'. This was particularly unfortunate, as Poiret was actually employed by Worth at the time. Jean-Philippe was a product of the grand style of couture laid down by Charles Frederick, his father, who was 60

Paul Poiret chose a young, unknown artist, Paul Iribe, to illustrate his catalogue of fashions in 1908, Les Robes de Paul Poiret. *The clothes shocked the couture establishment, but the drawings inspired a generation of fashion artists who followed the simple but arresting style.*

years old and a venerable figure in the world of fashion when Poiret was born, but Jean Philippe's partner and brother, Gaston, was on Poiret's side, and saw the need for change. Gaston said, in an oft-quoted remark, that while Maison Worth catered to the customer with a taste for truffles, it was high time they opened an annexe selling *pommes frites*.

Paul Poiret, who in appearance looked like a prosperous Norman farmer in his Sunday best and in need of a shave, was a veritable *enfant terrible* whose contribution to fashion, however, was considerable and long-lasting. He was the first couturier to promote fashion objectively as an art form in its own right, an entity, a medium of expression irrespective of the bodies which the clothes adorned. It is true that his wife—like Worth's wife Marie—was both his model and inspiration, and her lean and then unfashionable figure suited his aims, coinciding as it did with the tubular cycle. But Poiret was subversive to current ideals and he designed for the future.

Both Worth and Poiret had flair, some would say genius, but where Worth had exercised restraint, Poiret had no such qualms, and was an ardent publicist and showman. In keeping with the *zeitgeist* of emancipation, this stocky, bearded, avuncular figure was the liberator of women's bodies. If he didn't actually banish the corset, as some claim, he at least loosened it, allowing the waist to return to normal, dressing women in a sheath dress that hung down from the shoulders. Many saw Poiret's high-waisted style as a startling innovation, but it merely echoed the Empire line of exactly a century before; that which had introduced the first tubular cycle was now reintroducing the second. 'In a real sense,' said Young, 'fashion is evolution without destination.'

The war against the corset

The renaissance of the *mode à la grecque* was deliberate, but where the dresses of the earlier style were Indian muslins, Poiret now used silk, satin and velvet, in strong colours and combinations. 'The reds, the royal blues, and the oranges and lemons made all the rest sit up and take notice,' Poiret recalled in his autobiography, 'and my sunburst of pastels brought a new dawn.' He set off the dresses with motifs and accessories sympathetic to Art Nouveau, and hair styles were short (like the Titus cut of 1800, and Jeanne Récamier's curls) worn with a bandeau of silk or crêpe.

If these dresses were 'dishcloths', *Vogue's* Paris correspondent was keen to promote them nonetheless. 'Be grateful that we are at present enjoying not only the most salutary but the most artistic style since the Greek era, in which we are neither sloping nor square but just graceful human beings.'

This Hellenic style, attributed to Poiret, had been in existence at least three years before Poiret opened his first shop in the Rue Auber. In fact the *Directoire* line, as it was also known, appeared in the late 1880s in anticipation of the return of the tubular cycle, but only in tea gowns and some evening dresses, and the loose, flowing robes of the Aesthetic Movement. This brave attempt to break away from the stately formality of Victorian fashions was part of the artistic reform begun by the Pre-Raphaelites. In dress it appeared as an idealized blend of renais-

A mink coat from the Paris modes of 1900, with matching hat and muff, and collar lined with lace. Furs were included in couture collections, and a number of couturiers trained as furriers.

sance and classical styles, in muted colours and pastel shades as promoted by the fabric designs of Arthur Liberty.

The movement was also led by several artists and literary figures, notably Walter Crane and William Morris; Pater, Swinburne and Oscar Wilde. Wilde, in his velvet and silk dress coat and breeches, patent leather pumps with bows, and silk stockings, was singled out and parodied in Gilbert and Sullivan's opera *Patience*—a satire on the movement—as the 'Francesca da Rimini, miminy, piminy, *Je-ne-sais-quoi* young man.'

Although most women wore the tight-laced corset, there were alternatives. Even in 1902 the magazine *The Queen* praised a 'little Empire corset—or *ceinture*—(which) merely covers the bust, and is held by shoulder straps, and over this the Empire *toilette* hangs to perfection.' *The Lady* confirmed that 'Waists are considered trifles to which all sensible women have said goodbye.'

The war which Poiret waged upon the corset was directed at those women who continued to favour the nipped-in waist and to whom he offered a slim corset of elastic which started below the bust, rode smoothly over the hips to the suspenders, giving a gentle and undulating line. 'This may,' said *The Queen*, 'be called the Poiret figure, for it is certainly in his salons that the boneless corset is most in vogue.'

It became clear to other couturiers in 1900 that radical changes were due. One such couturier was Gaston Worth, another was Madeleine Vionnet, who claimed to have liberated the bodies of the fashion models from corsets when she was working for Doucet in 1903. The straight-line, tubular cycle which more or less coincided with the new century needed a straight-line foundation, and since it was far too radical a move actually to discard corsets altogether, the corset underwent the necessary metamorphosis. The immutable laws that govern the progress of fashion were being exploited by those couturiers who happened to be in the right place at the right time.

Riots and insanities — The oriental influence

What exactly did Paul Poiret achieve? He didn't invent the Empire line, since it was there already. He did not banish the corset, although he did play a part in changing its shape, but this might have occurred anyway in keeping with the linear style of the tubular dress shape. What he did do was establish an art form using the current imagery and the motifs of modern art as opposed to the traditional, and to sever the ties that bound fashion to hierarchy. He allied himself to those artists who were staging a revolt against established principles at a time when the Establishment was at its most defensive and vulnerable.

In government and military circles, the Dreyfus Affair was still echoing down the corridors of power. The works of the Impressionists, in artistic academic circles, were still a cause for scandal, since 27 pictures by artists Monet, Renoir, Degas, Cézanne and others had been rejected as unfit to be seen, let alone tolerated. But they could hardly ignore the fact that the anarchism of modern art was busily eroding the foundations of the art establishment. In *ateliers* across Paris, the 'wild beast' Fauves, the appalling Cubists, Braque and Picasso, who made statements like

What the well-dressed American lady wore when taking the dog for a walk—a Walking Suit, from the magazine The Delineator, *1905. The material is mixed-blue English suiting, and she wears an Eton-style bolero over her bodice.*

'Don't paint what you see, paint what you know to be there,' and the early Surrealism of Odilon Redon, were busy kicking away the props.

More was to follow. In 1909 Diaghilev brought the Ballet Russe to Paris. Although there were enough native musicians with an apparent preference for discord, such as Ravel, Satie and Debussy, to offend the ears of the more staid concert-goers, the Russians actually imported one of their own in the shape of Igor Stravinsky. At the performance of *The Firebird*, and subsequently *Petrushka*, Paris audiences were in turns shocked, appalled, delighted and made aware that here, new and violent forces were

Poiret's designs from 1908 in Les Robes de Paul Poiret. *The work of this revolutionary couturier was beginning to be taken seriously, and Poiret introduced his second catalogue,* Les Choses de Paul Poiret, *in 1911.*

One of the ballet designs by Leon Bakst for Diaghilev's Ballet Russe, in 1909. Bakst's vibrant, powerful drawings considerably influenced fabric design in the early 1900s, and his costumes for such performances as Sheherazade were made up by the houses of Paquin and Worth.

within their midst. The riots that followed Stravinsky's *Rite of Spring* confirmed their worst fears, but some of the magic rubbed off, especially the wonderfully powerful designs of Leon Bakst, whose oriental-style costumes and sets endowed the receptive art circles of Paris with a renewed enthusiasm for the East.

Eastern influences inspired Poiret's turbans, his kimonos and Japanese parasols and his Russian peasant blouses. They inspired, too, the drawings of demure, slant-eyed maidens *à la japonaise* by Poiret's friend and admirer, the fashion artist George Lepape. The craze for Japanese styles had actually waxed and waned for over fifty years, and only made a noticeable impression on fabrics and styles—the kimono sleeves for example—during the first decade of the twentieth century. I am referring here to mainstream fashion and not the sundry dress reform movements such as the Aesthetics, with their preference for Liberty prints. In fact, during the 1880s, the Aesthetics were pointing the way which later couturiers would follow.

There was a rather confusing mishmash of styles and intentions. Orthodox, everyday fashions finally caught up with Japanese styles about 1908–10, and with Art Nouveau in 1911–12. The *Directoire* high waist appeared on day dresses from 1911 (and fell back to normal in 1919) while Poiret, Paquin, Worth and others were showing their high waists and oriental styles from 1910 through to 1918. Lucile, the principal London couturier, had designed *Directoire* dresses in 1907, and was still showing similar styles in 1918. In some of her designs it is hard to judge who had the idea first – she or Poiret.

From 1908 the skirt hem rose to reveal the ankles and the popular buttoned or laced ankle boots. As the hem rose, the 'S' bend began to straighten and there was a fashion for long gowns that buttoned from neck to hem. This was when Poiret showed a dress slit from knee to ankle which provoked, from *Le Figaro*, 'These gowns are, without a shadow of a doubt, the worst of all the recent insanities.' But of all his designs, it is the famous hobble skirt that, curiously enough, had the greatest and most widespread impact on couture and mainstream fashions.

Eagerly, women slipped into gowns that rendered movement difficult if not impossible. The hobble came in at about the time that waistlines began to rise in 1911, and seems to have persisted beyond 1914. It was worn with dignity at Longchamps and Auteuil; it was worn even by suffragettes, who plainly did not consider the inconvenience of fashions detrimental to their cause, symbolizing though it did restrictions to their liberty. They were made fashionable when Emily Pankhurst in England, and Cornelia Otis Skinner in America, joined the movement.

The rat, the bra and the permanent wave

Dress styles have little to do with social trends, and fashions do not reflect discontents. For a brief period during World War I, skirts filled out, hemlines rose to an unprecedented height and patch pockets appeared on day dresses, but it is hard to link these minor trends to cataclysmic events. Fashion doesn't need world wars or major market depressions to effect styles. All that is required is a gesture made by some figure in the public eye. Poiret was launched when the actress Réjane began wearing his dresses, just as the Princess Metternich's patronage had launched Worth. When Isadora Duncan appeared with bobbed hair, and Irene Castle revealed her short *coiffure* created by her husband cum dancing-partner Vernon, women rushed to the hairdressers.

They did not do so when a German hairdresser, Karl Nessler, opened his salon in London, in 1904. It was not so much that Nessler's coiffures were unappealing, it was more to do with the fact that his hairstyles took twelve hours to complete, and cost a great deal of money. They were, in a word, 'permanent'. Under the name of Charles Nestlé (if it's French it's fashionable) he launched the first Nestlé Permanent Waving technique. Nestlé opened in New York in 1908 and, in the first year, the service attracted a mere 18 women, perhaps the only ones who could afford the fee of one thousand dollars.

For the time being women would have to make do with crimping irons, 'transformations' (as wigs were called) and the

The spirit of the age. In the early part of the twentieth century the zeitgeist *reflected some degree of female emancipation, embodied by the American dancer Isadora Duncan, whose barefoot, free-style dancing in flowing draperies helped to promote liberation from the corset, buttoned boots, huge hats and tight skirts that women endured.*

rat . . . This was a pad of false hair which gave added height to the then fashionable pompadour style. It was decorated with brooches, pins, combs and whatever came in handy. For their part, men kept their hair short, but, while the more mature man retained his beard or moustache or both, young men shaved. Soon, the young men would endure a different kind of uniformity when they responded to the demands of Lord Kitchener and Uncle Sam. Labour-saving America was meanwhile setting the pace that everyone else was likely to follow. The 240,000th Model T Ford had rolled off the production line, and a lady in New York had just invented the brassière.

Mary Phelps Jacob, later Caresse Crosby, came from a family of inventors, having descended from Robert Fulton who devised a type of steamboat. 'I can't say that the brassière will ever take as great a place in history as the steamboat,' she admitted, 'but I did invent it, and perpetual motion has always just been around the corner.' To many millions of women, the brassière was a much greater invention than any steamboat (quite a few men might agree) and Mary Phelps filed her patent No. 1,115,674 in November 1914.

To free herself from the grip of the corset, Mary Jacob made a prototype bra from two handkerchiefs, a length of pink ribbon, and thread to stitch them together. With the patent to her 'Back-less Brassière' as she called it, Mary Jacob approached through a friend Warner Brothers Corset Company, who offered her $15,000; experts have since estimated that the contract was worth $20 million, but the inventor, as the heiress Caresse Crosby, probably would not have needed the money.

Before the brassière reached the stage of mass production in the 1920s and 1930s, women wore a corset belt, made principally of elastic, combined with a brassière. This corselette was admirably suited to the delicate, sheath-like dresses of satin and velvet, with their low *décolletage*, designed by Poiret.

'Vulgar, wicked and ugly!' — Couturiers on tour

By 1911 there was no stopping the *enfant terrible* couturier in his bid for world recognition. Attired in beige motoring coats, he and Denise Poiret embarked in a chauffeur-driven Renault on the conquest of Europe; his collections, models and a lecture film followed by train. Frankfurt, Vienna, Bucharest, Budapest, and finally St Petersburg, fell to the Poirets. Now, if Napoleon had been a couturier . . .

Poiret's kimono coats, lampshade tunics, and the remarkably successful pantaloon gown — which Jean Worth described as 'vulgar, wicked and ugly!' — somewhat overshadowed the efforts of other couturiers such as Redfern, Doucet, Chéruit and Callot Soeurs, but not Paquin. In the same year, 1911, Poiret succumbed to his passion for fashion and flamboyance and held one of his fancy-dress balls. Choosing an oriental theme and calling it 'The Thousand and Second Night', he attired himself in a caftan and turban. For Denise, he designed a lampshade tunic, wired at the hem with a gold fringe, a bodice of white chiffon with matching pantaloons and a gold turban like his, topped by a white aigrette. Lest it be thought that Poiret held a monopoly on the new vogue

A chiffon afternoon dress of 1910, when waistlines were beginning to rise, and hemlines reluctantly followed to reveal the barest glimpse of an ankle. Skirts were becoming slimmer, anticipating the hobble of 1911.

for oriental styles, Mme Paquin engaged Bakst and Paul Iribe, the protégé of Poiret, to design for her. She, too, went on tour with her collection, following the Poirets to America. Innovative though Poiret clearly was, Mme Paquin's clothes were more practical and above all softly and expensively romantic, in subtle pastel shades —'a harmony of nuances' and 'a fairyland' said press reviews.

Paquin shared with London couturier Lucile (who was also Lady Duff Gordon) a shrewd grasp of business matters and a sharp eye for publicity. Paquin opened in London, New York and Buenos Aires; Lucile in New York and Paris. Lucile, somewhat egotistically, claimed 'I had a message for the women I dressed. I was the first dressmaker to bring joy and romance into clothes. I was a pioneer.' In those days *all* the couturiers were pioneers, but what mattered most was the ability to adapt to social change, to survive through world wars and economic depressions, and above all to keep pace with the fluctuations of fashion. Poiret would not survive, he was too theatrical and too impractical.

In total contrast, there was a young designer who opened a small hat shop in the seaside resort of Deauville in 1911, whose clothes were destined to endure for over fifty years. Her name was Gabrielle Chanel, and as 'Coco' Chanel probably holds the record as the longest surviving couturier, whose fashions were still in vogue, and in *Vogue*, up to the time of her death in 1971.

Madame Paquin's elegant salon in 1910, in the Rue de la Paix, in close proximity to Maison Worth. Dubbed 'The Queen of Paris Fashion' by the French press, she ran the next most prosperous and influential couture establishment to that of Worth. She was always 'Madame Paquin' and although, presumably, she possessed a first name, it is never disclosed.

Chapter 7

COUTURE GOES PUBLIC

1914-1920

The last garment to survive the Victorian and Edwardian eras of fashion were the tea gowns, or 'Dainty Tea Frocks', as their advertisers liked to call them. They were also known as 'Rest Frocks', a name which reflects the age of leisure about to be blown away by World War I. The War had little effect on fashion, but skirts became looser and fuller, and legs were revealed as never beore. The modernization of fashion began, not so much with Poiret's freer styles, but when mass-production techniques produced ready-to-wear suits and dresses, based on Paris designs. The most noticeable feature in the first decades of the twentieth century was the importance of hats. Hats for both men and women, hats with feathers, veils, artificial flowers; big hats, floppy hats, small hats, silly hats, military styles, they completed the total ensemble that now included the handbag and the neatly rolled umbrella. Under the hat, hair was worn short in the manner started by Irene Castle and Isadora Duncan, encouraged by the craze for sport and the general movement towards careers for women. It was a way of life perfectly suited to the aims of Chanel. 'The First War made me,' she was to say later.
'In 1919 I woke up famous.'

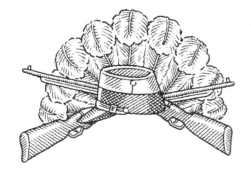

When Paul Poiret invented the hobble skirt in 1910, and effectively cramped the style of every woman who aspired to be fashionable (though he had freed her from the 'S' shaped corset), he revealed the powerful influence that one man's ideas could have on everyday, mainstream fashion. Apart from Worth's Princess line, which was not all that adaptable to mass production, the hobble was the first design in which *haute couture* had shown the extent of its authority, and the way it can often affect what we wear down to the shape of a button. Poiret was the first couturier to impose that authority in an individual way. Whereas Worth designed exclusive dresses that suited a particular client, Poiret designed clothes that expressed his own, personal view of fashion as an art form.

Some of his designs were whimsical and impractical but popular. The hobble was one, the 'lampshade' dress—a sort of ghost crinoline that swung around the hips—was another, as were the pantaloon gowns of 1910 and the tiered dress of 1914. But at least they were entirely original, they were different from anything seen before, and thus Poiret, along with Chanel, paved the way for the democratization of couture styles.

Manufacturers pay close attention to the declarations of couturiers. Before fashion designs were protected by copyright laws, some unscrupulous dress manufacturers simply plundered the designers' work, pirating not only the designs themselves, but even the labels. A few still do this, and risk litigation with a defiant 'copy and be damned' attitude. But the risk isn't only that of a law suit, for the manufacturer has to gauge public taste as surely as the couturier—more so if he doesn't want a factory stocked with unsaleable garments on his hands. Today, the couturiers and manufacturers (with the aid of the fashion press) stimulate, and are in advance of, public demand, but when Poiret introduced the hobble skirt, production had to supply the demand, perforce belatedly. Anyway, the hobble stimulated wonderful controversy, which was good for business.

Was it also popular because it allowed women to wield power by endorsing it and by flaunting tradition, or because women enjoyed the role of being helpless and vulnerable? Whatever style took the public's fancy it became clear that the couturier offered a new vigour in dress, and a source of inspiration that had turned the somewhat plodding progress of fashion on its head; Poiret and his unorthodox, colourful designs had pointed the way to the future. But it isn't only the couturiers who determine the styles of clothes that we wear.

Fashion is perpetually sensitive to the kaleidoscopic patterns registered by the shifts, changes and caprices of everyday life, exploiting the latest fads to its own purpose. In the decade before World War I, America was dancing the Boston Two-Step, the Turkey Trot, the Bunny Hug and an exciting new dance called the Tango, which inspired the shoe industry to produce suitable footwear—the cuban heel of 1904, and the tango shoe of 1913 with its louis heel and laces around the ankles.

A potentially versatile design, such as a zouave or a bolero jacket, a skirt, hat, sleeve or even a glove, can be recycled to produce a garment that has at least the appearance of being

The hobble skirt, or, as the French called it, 'la jupe entravée'.

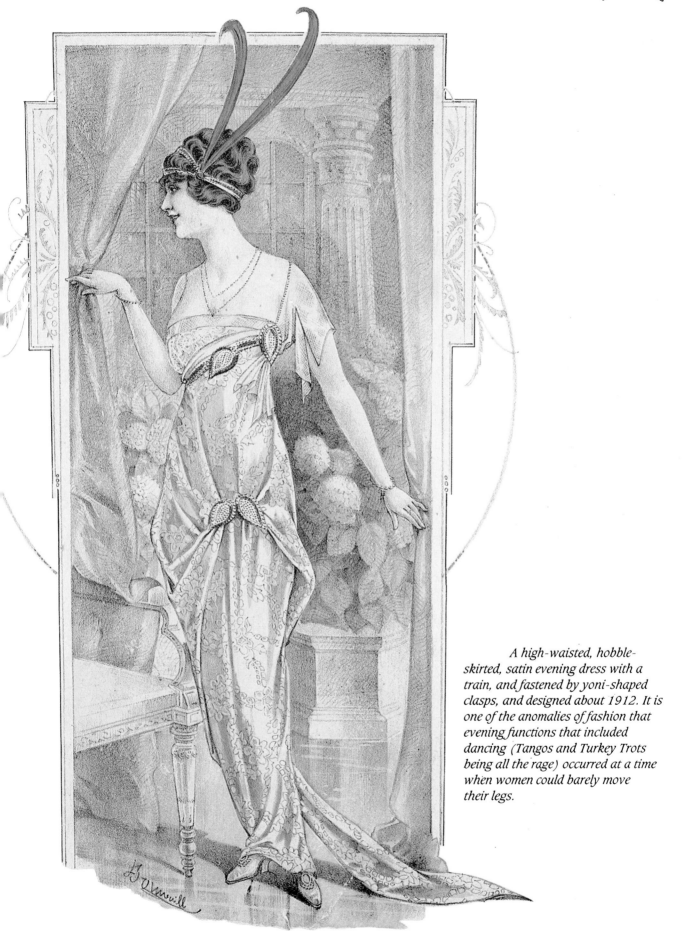

A high-waisted, hobble-skirted, satin evening dress with a train, and fastened by yoni-shaped clasps, and designed about 1912. It is one of the anomalies of fashion that evening functions that included dancing (Tangos and Turkey Trots being all the rage) occurred at a time when women could barely move their legs.

The Yellow Dress, one of Poiret's 'dishcloths', — un torchon *as Jean-Philippe Worth contemptuously called his employee's designs. Poiret was not an ideal employee, and soon set up his own house, creating a collection illustrated in his book* Les Choses de Paul Poiret *in 1911, with drawings by Georges Lepape, from which this picture is taken.*

novel—upon this premise are a million patterns produced. The keen response from a legion of women who desired nothing more than to be moderately chic, even if not aspiring to the dizzy heights of couture, was great. The average woman—if there ever was such a person—bought her dresses from department stores— with tango shoes to match. The stores had much improved the output of their dressmaking departments since the time of Worth, and included a skilled alteration service advertising dresses that were 'ready to wear except joining back seam of skirt'. This bespoke element gave a faint touch of exclusiveness and a personal input—like adding an egg to a cake mix.

With more young women in work and more husbands having an increased income, women of all classes and occupations could expect to be attired in a respectably fashionable style. As Prudence Glynn said, 'Not so long ago (they) would have thought themselves fortunate to be adequately clothed.' While a wealthier class of woman could afford to go to a private dressmaker, the rest studied home dressmaking and bought paper patterns. As the design and cut of clothes became simpler, so the consumer became more confident in her skills; her requirements were supplied by specialist pattern firms such as Butterick, McCalls and Weldons, and by the new fashion magazines. *Vogue* published patterns, and in the 1920s launched the *Vogue Pattern Book*. At the lower end of the market were such magazines as *La Nouvelle Mode* in France and, in England, *Home Notes* which published weekly mail-order dressmaking patterns and intriguing features titled 'Is Kissing Doomed?' and 'The Management of Men'.

The home dressmaking boom

There were few dressmaking books before the nineteenth century, then came a number of specialist works, such as Madame Burtel's *Art de la Couturière en Robes* in 1826. The slow and labour-intensive process of dressmaking was crying out for mechanization, and in 1830 the first signs of advancement appeared with Thimmonier's sewing machine in France, followed by those of Walter Hunt and Elias Howe in America. The most successful was Isaac Singer's patent of 1851, and within a decade Singer machines were being mass produced in New Jersey, and the sewing machine was every girl's best friend. By 1875 the publication of *The Complete Dressmaker for the Million* was assured of a huge and eager following.

In Britain every Singer machine came with a book *Easy Dressmaking* by Florence White. Were the author better known she would rank alongside Mrs Beeton as a great cookery writer and journalist, as well as being a dressmaker. Florence emerges from the late Victorian age, through the Edwardian period and into the twentieth century as a remarkable figure. Cruelly treated in childhood by a fairytale wicked stepmother, the thin, infirm, one-eyed Florence struggled to survive as a dressmaker. After becoming a social worker in East London, then an English teacher in Paris (where she met Rodin) and a domestic servant in Cambridge, when she began writing for the *Cambridge Evening News*, she became *The Times* cookery writer and author of two classic works on food. As a reporter for the *Edinburgh Evening News* she was perhaps the first and only correspondent to despatch fashion bulletins by carrier pigeon.

In her autobiography, Florence White gives details of fashions and morals in the days when 'sex was taboo' and 'housemaids wore nightgowns of unbleached calico, cut on strictly utilitarian lines. The sleeves of their chemises consisted of a square of calico, with a square gusset underneath which, being put in on the cross, ensured endless wear and tear and allowed for the expenditure of any amount of energy and elbow grease. I can assure you,' added Florence, 'that it was a fine art to be able to insert a gusset.'

The New Look for 1910, big hat, short hairstyle, neat, tailored appearance with less emphasis on the waist, and straight lines down to the ground. Skirts were pleated and some were provided with slits for freedom of movement—until the hobble arrived. Never before, or not since the Empire line, had fashion been so unreservedly simple.

Fabric cut on the cross is the same as bias cutting, a dressmaking technique that utilizes the full potential strength and stretch of the fabric. Each type of fabric possesses characteristics according to its natural weight, its texture, the structure of its fibres, and so on. All woven fabric has a grain, that is, the direction of the threads: the 'warp' forms the lengthways grain, the 'woof' or 'weft' the cross grain. Cloth cut on the straight grain has less flexibility than fabric cut at an angle—45 degrees across the grain—but the straight grain has the obvious advantage of strength and regularity, ideal, say, for a man's suit. If you cut on the bias, the cloth will give you a more fluid line, hugging the contours of the body, or draping in arranged folds, suitable for a long evening dress.

Jersey, silk, satin and crêpe respond wonderfully to bias cutting, a technique pioneered and perfected in couture styling by Madeleine Vionnet, whom some still honour as the finest of all couturiers (or rather, *couturières*)—and there are many contenders to the title. Vionnet cut entire dresses on the cross, where previously the technique had been used mainly for details such as belts, yokes and gussets. To give Florence White her due—and couturiers like to be given credit for their innovations—she seems to have done away with boned bodices in 1890, well before Poiret and Vionnet, using an arrangement of ribbons which kept the fullness of the bodice without the boned lining, one of the earliest, she says, of the 'shapeless dresses'.

Chanel's instant chic

Dressmaking was not a required skill for couturiers, however. Gabrielle Chanel—the *couturière* whose appeal lasted longer than any other in the history of fashion—*couldn't* sew, nor could Paul Poiret. Cutting is the very essence of couture and fashion. Cutting is sculpting and fitting the material to the body, and Chanel was a genius with the scissors. 'All you have to do,' she explained, 'is to subtract. You have your cloth with length and width—what you have to do is cut.'

Chanel, known to her intimates as Coco, and to everyone else as 'Mademoiselle', had two watchwords: simplicity and understatement. 'Nothing makes a woman look older than obvious expensiveness', she said, 'I still dress as I always did, like a schoolgirl.' Yet it was her *boyishness* that led to her inimitable style, for she designed clothes that suited her own, spare frame or snatched up, *ad hoc*, odd garments to wear according to her whim. The fact is that Chanel had the great gift of an inherent personal style and whatever she wore became instant chic. She was also, as she herself admitted, in the right place at the right time.

Dates and places in the life of Coco Chanel are somewhat vague, a confusion of fact and fiction which is part of the Chanel legend and to which she deliberately contributed. What seems certain is that she was born in 1883 (three years after Patou) and the date of her first business enterprise was about 1909. She opened a hat shop in Paris under the auspices of her lover Etienne Balsan, and later, backed by her second paramour, the Englishman Arthur 'Boy' Capel, she opened another hat shop where she sold hats stripped of adornment—hats burdened with fruit,

In spite of the new, clean lines there was a decided reluctance to shed the towering, statuesque style of the Edwardian lady, although Poiret had shown the way ahead in Paris. 'Picture hats' were the biggest ever in 1910, practically insupportable and equalled only by the size of the muffs women carried.

'Faune', designed by Poiret in 1919 and worn by his wife Denise. It has a backless bodice and turban, both in gold fabric, while the skirt has a gold fringe and is trimmed with monkey-fur fabric, and worn with a long-trained cloak. Very theatrical, very Poiret, and hardly in keeping with the mood of the times.

flowers and feathers then being fashionable—and wore one of them herself (she was the perfect promoter of her own styles) with a sweater and a string of pearls. She refused to wear corsets, and designed clothes that, as she put it, she 'could jump straight into'. The contrast with the high-waisted, long skirts of 1910 must have been startling. Mused Poiret, 'We ought to have been on our guard against that boyish head. It was going to give us every kind of shock . . . *coiffures*, sweaters, and jewels and boutiques.'

Chanel, in particular, was able to exploit her own personal flair and chic to promote her own fashions, especially as she moved in high society—French, Russian and English. In 1914 she opened her couture business in 81, Rue Cambon, conveniently close to the Ritz. She was still there in 1971 and had become a legend. In her reminiscences about Chanel, her friend Claude Baillén tells us that, 'It was she who launched the things we like now—the once despised jersey, the little black dress, beige, navy-blue and white, real pockets, comfortable coats, bell-bottomed trousers and artificial jewellery.' Chanel's simple designs of 1916, a jersey-fabric jumper cut across the hips, with a matching skirt and blouse tied with a sash, show her casual approach and her concept of the ensemble.

We can regard the first two decades of the twentieth century as the most radical and significant period in women's fashions—the most fundamental breakaway from tradition—and generated by Poiret and Chanel. But where women sought change, men remained obstinately conservative. Said Young, 'The tendency to cling to established forms with the minimum amount of yearly change seems clearly a pronounced feature of masculine clothes that has no counterpart in women's fashions.'

Certainly the women were the more progressive of the sexes. Men's fashions were stick-in-the-mud clothes against which the mercurial nature of women's fashions, and attitudes, could be measured and compared. Women now played golf, smoked cigarettes, drove cars, and some intrepid ladies—including Chanel—wore trousers! Said the American journalist Ida Tarbell doubtfully, 'Is woman making a man of herself?' The answer was a ringing 'No!' especially so since the modern man was hardly the model of chic, let alone ton.

The pre-war conservative male wore a three-piece suit of matching trousers, single-breasted jacket and waistcoat; Oxford shoes, shirt with a soft turned-down collar, a tie, bowler hat or boater. It was not acceptable for a man to go bare-headed, even less acceptable to wear his shirt open-necked. Ties continued to be muted and sincere, a black silk tie was worn with a tuxedo, white tie with evening dress. Hair was worn short, often parted in the centre, and as a general rule men were clean shaven.

Now that the rules were being challenged, at least in women's fashions, it is strange that the lead was not taken in America, with its huge polyglot pioneering society. Here was the opportunity to wrest the supremacy from Paris, but the trouble was that Americans, lacking any real indigenous cultural roots, did not have the self-confidence to take on the cultivated French—

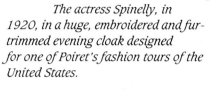

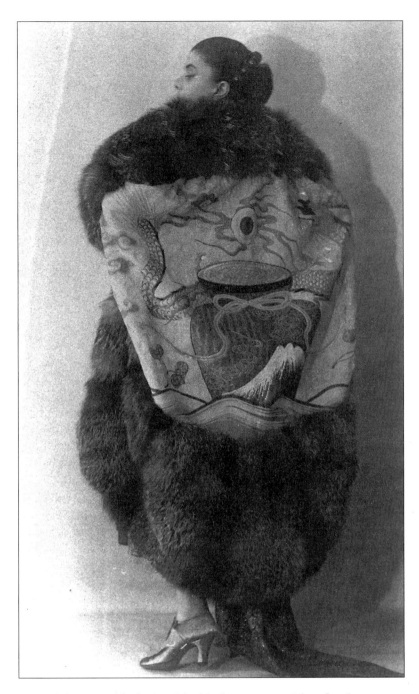

The actress Spinelly, in 1920, in a huge, embroidered and fur-trimmed evening cloak designed for one of Poiret's fashion tours of the United States.

or Parisians—with their critical judgement. Neither for that matter did the English.

The French capital won its epithet 'Gay Paree' by virtue of its vigorous pursuit of life, where intellectual and hedonistic goals were given equal weight, and where good taste in fashion, as in food, was deemed of great cultural importance. Prudence Glynn, in her book *In Fashion*, points out that the British regarded fashion with suspicion and were impatient of its 'constant capricious change. Poised uneasily between France and America, Britain never accepted good fashion as an integral part of civilized life as did the French, nor was it peddled by quite such high-pressure methods as the Americans had developed.'

Americans were ahead of the game in terms of advertising and mass production and were content to look to Paris (as everyone did) for originality. This is not to say that the French had

Poiret, second from the left, with staff and models from his couture house on the feast day of the couturiers. The girl standing in the centre is the token 'St Catherine' for the day. Anyway, it provided Poiret with an opportunity for dressing up, something which he rarely missed.

a total monopoly of couture, for there were a few foreigners who could match them in flair and style, stitch by stitch, seam for seam. There was Lady Duff Gordon, originally Lucy Sutherland and Canadian, who began in London as the *couturière* Lucy.

Romance and opulence — Lucile Ltd

Lucy had three advantages over other aspiring *couturières*: she was the elder sister of the romantic and successful novelist Elinor Glyn, and she married a title — Sir Cosmo Duff Gordon — which gave her trading a certain cachet. Her third advantage was that she was a natural publicist, and being the sister of the notorious Elinor was no bad thing for business. In 1907 the literary world, and also the average reader, was shocked and scandalized by Elinor's novel *Three Weeks*. It sold two million copies and provoked the jingle:

> Would you like to sin
> On a tiger skin
> With Elinor Glyn?
> Or would you prefer
> To err
> With her
> On some other fur?

As business prospered, Lucy took the more imposing title of Lucile Ltd and opened, in the 1890s, in Old Burlington Street. Lucile opted for the romantic look, romantic and opulent with rich draped silks and satins. She designed for the discerning and theatrical dresser, even down to her client's underwear.

When her income topped a dizzy £40,000 a year she broadened her horizons and opened in New York and Paris. In her London branch she installed a young designer who eventually graduated to her couture house in Paris. This was Edward Molyneux, who was to become one, of the great couturiers of the Twenties and Thirties, opening his own house in 1919. Lucile, red-headed and quick-tempered, and possessed of a certain *folie de grandeur*, kept a watchful eye on Poiret and incorporated, as did others, some of his ideas into her designs. She was justly accused of having pirated designs from the young Norman Hartnell but couture piracy was, and is, par for the course.

Lucile made a permanent contribution to the world of fashion by developing and promoting the concept of the mannequin, the fashion model. She was the first to produce a stagey, theatrical presentation and her collections were enhanced by tall, confident-looking English girls parading to the strains of a small orchestra. Lucile's most famous mannequins were Dolores, who became a showgirl in Florenz Ziegfeld's Follies in New York in 1917, and the model Sumurun who quit Lucile for Captain Molyneux.

Lucile was furious at Sumurun's defection, especially since Molyneux was her ex-protégé and employee, running her Paris house. Years later, Sumurun told fashion writer Brigid Keenan, 'You couldn't stand up against Madame, she was a real power. When she discovered I wanted to go and work for the Captain she took me between finger and thumb, turned me round to face the door and said, "You . . . whom I have treated like a sister—GO".' Poiret, taking a leaf out of Lucile's book, hired mannequins and took them to New York. Some years later Jean Patou, going one better, went to New York and hired leggy American girls to come to Paris as mannequins for his shows.

Silk, satin and lace—Mixed fortunes for the couture houses

World War I had little effect on the progress of the basic fashion cycle, but couture houses closed down, and Chanel, Vionnet, Patou and others had to suspend their services. Lucile's Paris branch closed when Edward Molyneux joined the British Army. Paul Poiret, with a suitably histrionic touch, declared that 'France needs men today, not artists!' and enlisted in the French infantry along with the Worth brothers. Poiret was ordered to learn how to sew buttons on army greatcoats, which he promptly re-designed. The coats, he claimed, used far too much material, and Poiret spent the remainder of the War trying to get his new design into production. It is a pity that he failed. To have the entire French army dressed by Poiret might have been no bad thing for morale!

During the mid-War years, 1916–17, skirts had assumed a bell-shaped profile out of keeping with the straight-line trend. Such variations are not uncommon in fashion cycles, and are sometimes the expression of one couturier's mood or vision, such as the neat-waisted, flaring skirt of Jeanne Lanvin which boasted

Lucile, or Lady Duff Gordon, rose to fame with her 'Merry Widow' hat, which she designed for the opera singer Lily Elsie. Huge and ornate, it was typical of Edwardian extravagance—and was widely copied.

127

the highest ever hemline—to mid calf. For two years, skirts were full, with tiers of frills and flounces. The abrupt raising of the hemline might also have been the result of women's temporary release from male criticism. In any event, the smart woman wore a bouffant skirt with patent leather lace-up boots, 'the skirt five or six inches off the ground, the height of the boot being eight inches, and no well-dressed woman will wear a gown that covers her boot less than two inches.'

After the War the fortunes of several couturiers declined, the most notable being Poiret in Paris and Lucile in London. Like the exotic Poiret, Lucile's style was too theatrical and downright expensive to survive the shorn Twenties and the jerking Jazz Age. But it had been great while it lasted. 'For me there was a positive intoxication in taking yards of shimmering silks, laces airy as gossamer and lengths of ribbons delicate and rainbow coloured,' she said in 1932, in her memoirs *Discretions and Indiscretions*, 'and fashioning garments so lovely that they might have been worn by some princess in a fairy tale.' Cinderella perhaps, for Lucile was a superb and extravagant designer of evening wear during a period when evening engagements were the highpoint of an active social life; a period never to be recaptured with the same degree of opulence.

The transient nature of taste and fashion has created the belief that couturiers have, at best, a working life of 15 years; as fashions decline, so does the couturier. William Reville Terry and Irene Rossiter, as Reville and Rossiter, became Court dressmakers to Queen Mary, and suffered a similar fate to that of Lucile. The splended publicity and wealthy clientele, the pomp and circumstance of Court fashion must have stifled any *avant-garde* notions that William Reville, as the chief designer, might have possessed.

Some fashion designers, though, have a timeless quality. Grès for one, Vionnet for another, because they remained firmly dedicated to the classical linear style that so perfectly suits the tubular cycle. Their designs successfully span generation gaps of several decades so that the dresses created by Chanel, with her commonsense approach, for example, enabled her to make her famous come-back in 1954.

Much the same can be said of Fortuny. Marinaro Fortuny was a painter from a family of painters, and left Spain to settle in Venice as he greatly admired the Renaissance artists. The Renaissance influence can be seen in the textile patterns that Fortuny designed. His interest in couture came about through his involvement with theatre design and stage costume—he dressed Sarah Bernhardt and Isadora Duncan. He dressed Greta Garbo and Eleanora Duse. He also dressed himself. Photographs of Fortuny in his later years show him looking rather like Poiret occasionally did—bearded, with a turban and Middle Eastern robes.

Fortuny made a unique contribution to fashion, since he was the only couturier to patent a fabric. While you cannot patent a style—or couldn't just after the War—nor a method of cutting such as Vionnet's bias technique, you can, of course, patent a manufacturing process. Fortuny invented a method of exceptionally fine pleating, probably achieved by hot-pressing the wet silk or satin material, and holding it under pressure while drying.

The free-style dresses of 1916, surprisingly modern and comparable to the flaring skirts and dirndls of the early 1950s. Flounced petticoats helped to give the required fullness. Flounces and frills were also a decorative feature of skirts at the time.

When worn it formed long, elegant drapery, and inspired his most famous creation, Delphos, based on the design of the Greek chiton (tunic) — a recurring source of ideas in couture.

Delphos was an evening dress of pleated satin that hung straight from the shoulders to the floor where it spread outwards like an inflorescence to form a neat circle around the feet. The simple neckline was held by a drawstring. To wear with the dress he designed a kimono-style jacket bearing a hand-printed metallic

A Delphos evening dress by Marinaro Fortuny, rolled in a bundle in order to preserve the pleats and the nature of the fabric. Fortuny's technique remains a mystery — experts still don't know how he created such a finely pleated textile, and the secret died with him in 1949.

129

pattern of Renaissance motifs. There is a fine example, from which my description is derived, in London's Victoria and Albert Museum. It could be worn today, and in fact Fortuny enjoyed a revival in the late 1970s through to 1980.

Furs for all — The fur boom in the Twenties

After the War three army captains surrendered their uniforms and returned to the more familiar attire of couturiers. They were Poiret, Patou, and Molyneux (who retained his rank for the rest of his career and was known in couture circles as 'The Captain'). By 1919 the waistline had returned from high to normal (though it was shortly due to descend) and the parasol was an essential accessory. But the most noticeable fashion accessory was fur. Soldiers returning home said that the first things they'd noticed were the shorter skirts, and the fact that so many women were wearing fur coats.

Practically everything with fur and four legs was fair game — skunk, beaver, musquash, moleskin, opossum and coney. Even a woman of modest means could afford a fur stole, or a fur wrap of fox, worn casually across the shoulders, a fur which usually took the form of the entire animal including the head, legs and brush or tail. Glass eyes were set in the head, while underneath the snout was a sprung jaw of tortoise-shell, used as a clasp.

Fur had all but replaced jewellery, and, if you were smothered in furs and kept your mouth shut, fur disguised your origins. Gloria steals a mink coat in John O'Hara's novel *Butterfield 8*, and slips it over her practically naked body to walk across Washington Square in New York — many authors have acknowledged the erotic effect of fur. It is not known who designed the first couture fur coat, some say Paquin, others Doucet, but as a luxury item long associated with privilege and the sumptuary laws, it was an obvious addition to the couture world; both Patou and Lelong had trained as furriers. Yet by the Twenties fur was no longer quite so exclusive having broken the bounds of hierarchy and tradition.

Fashion itself had undergone swift and lasting changes — a glimpse of stocking as something shocking now only applied if it offended the purity of aesthetic taste rather than moral virtue. Patou said that he was offended by the sight of women who wore Chanel's short skirts because they revealed more than he desired to see at tea-time or, indeed, at any time of day.

Fashion was now responding to influences other than the couturier, so perhaps the short skirt celebrated the introduction of rayon (which went into commercial production just before World War I) which gave us artificial silk stockings and Celanese underwear. Sweaters were fashionable not just because of Chanel's example, but because women who had learned to knit socks for soldiers now turned their skills to knitted garments. Underwear, ideally suited to mass production and now advertised in a manner that, a decade or so before would have seemed almost pornographic, was coloured pale blue, pink and beige, and the fashionable figure now required no corsets. Dress was essentially unrestricted and simple in line and proportion, heralding the Jazz Age and the heyday of the flapper.

The fox fur (complete with snout, tail and legs) and fur trimmings of all kinds were prime fashion accessories in the early Twenties. Perhaps the fashion had something to do with women's new-found emancipation and greater confidence and self-awareness — and more money. Rather than having the fur side inside, women wanted the fur side outside: furs were for show, not for warmth.

Couture for the people—Seventh Avenue and mass production

One of the most important aspects of modern fashion is that of demand, supply and distribution, by wholesale dress manufacturers, from copies made from *haute couture* designs. *Haute couture* is, as we know, a luxury product designed by a handful of men and women for an exclusive clientele. But of course it doesn't end there, for couture styles, and copies based on original designs, are available to everyone, and at modest prices when compared to the cost of the original garment.

The mass production of ready-to-wear fashion became a reality only after World War I, and occurred through a number of influences. The first of these was the simplification of dress styles pioneered by Poiret's straight-line, tailored suits and tunic dresses in 1910, and by the gradual emergence of sportswear. These changes led to such innovations as the coat-frock, a long-sleeved, one-piece versatile garment sold in a variety of basic styles.

Factory mechanization, encouraged by the example of factory production methods used during the War, now exploited by the workforce of Jewish immigrant tailors, who had arrived in America at the end of the nineteenth century, further increased productivity. A back-up of semi-skilled, sweated labour workers, nearly all of them women, made a huge contribution—there were twenty thousand in the garment industry in New York's Seventh Avenue, centre of the industry, and in Britain there were 700,000 by 1910.

The Seventh Avenue manufacturers and the wholesalers in London paid Paris couture houses a copyright fee and supplied the stores with couture copies, some of which could be very

English couples in summer casuals on holiday. The date is uncertain, but in 1922 the waist had dropped to hip level. Skirt hems were just above the ankles in 1923 but rose again in 1925. Artificial silk stockings, made with the newly discovered rayon, were widely available, but white stockings were still worn with summer dresses. Those felt, French cloche hats in white were very fashionable in the early Twenties, and the two-piece jersey wool dress, introduced by Chanel (as worn by the lady on the right) were fashionable after 1920. It is certainly a ready-to-wear copy, and the picture was probably taken in 1923.

expensive. In the 1930s, £75 for a dress was well above the budget of the average woman, so most ready-to-wear dresses were 'free translations' of the current vogue, created by dress designers employed by the manufacturers, and skilled at adaptation and cutting corners, and substituting cheaper fabrics such as artificial silk, or rayon.

Elizabeth Ewing, in her book *The History of Twentieth Century Fashion*, describes the impact of rayon on mass production. 'It came into general use in fashion in the 1920s, with America taking the lead and the rest of the world following rapidly. By the mid Twenties pretty, inexpensive, smart dresses with the look and some of the glamour of silk were being factory-made for the popular market on both sides of the Atlantic. The girl of limited means could now enjoy being in fashion to a degree hitherto impossible. It was a tremendous innovation. The fashion trade saw and took advantage of this opportunity.'

The more expensive couture copies hinted at exclusiveness, and a particular model might be available only through one store although, of course, a number of different sizes might be stocked, although stores tended to order with the tall, lissome 'mannequin type' of woman in mind. Yet even prominent couturiers make mistakes. According to one story, eight women arrived at a party each wearing an identical dress by Marcel Rochas. To be rebuked by one international woman of influence would be enough to make many men leave town on urgent business, but to be reviled by eight . . .

The boyish woman – The new style arrives

In 1919 Jean Patou, Chanel and Edward Molyneux opened their respective couture establishments, followed in 1922 by Madeleine Vionnet, and in 1923 by Lucien Lelong. From now on the great names of *haute couture* would rule the fashion world. The two decades that spanned the turn of the century were remarkable in their output of couturiers: 1890 had begun with the births of Schiaparelli and Mainbocher, to be followed four years later by Molyneux and Balenciaga. The new century produced Norman Hartnell, Norman Norell and Gilbert Adrian, Charles James, Clare McCardell and Digby Morton, Christian Dior, Victor Steibel and Hardy Amies. There was also Jacques Fath, Madame Grés, Jean Patou, Lelong, Balmain, Rochas and Lanvin, and the long established houses such as Callot Soeurs and, of course, Worth.

In 1922 the waist dropped below the normal line to the hips. The most likely author of this novel style was Poiret (who had dressed Valentino for his film *The Sheik*). Skirts fell to just above the ankle. Dresses for day wear featured a rounded neckline popularized by Lucile, while sleeves were narrow at the top and filled out at the bottom around the wrist. Fashion was heading determinedly for the long, lean look which was to be maintained for the next 25 years.

'The old standard of dressing had gone forever', said Lucile, referring to the post-War years. 'Even the women who were noted as the best dressed in Europe had cut their dressmakers' bills to half the previous amounts.' Since most of the best-dressed women enjoyed legendary wealth, perhaps economy itself

Photographs of the American social scene in the Twenties and Thirties show the popularity of the tuxedo – the prime evening wear for young men. The 'tux' was named after Tuxedo Park in New York State, owned by the Lorillard family who made it a pleasure resort for the wealthy. A Tuxedo Club was established in the 1880s, and later one of the family, Griswold Lorillard, made the tail-less evening jacket fashionable in the early Twenties.

was fashionable, or perhaps they were no longer dressing at Lucile. 'The Rue de la Paix is nothing if not resourceful,' Lucile continues, 'and it brought in the idea of the "boyish woman". Here was the perfect answer to the problem. Slight figures covered with three yards of material'—remember the forty yards needed for some crinolines?— 'skirt ending just below the knees, tiny cloche hat trimmed with a band of ribbon. No woman, at least no women in civilization, could cost less to clothe.'

The current need or expression of brevity in style arose from the post-war feeling that the dearly held traditions and beliefs in our society had been blown away, along with the lives of millions of young men, so what was the point of maintaining old values and elegant manners of dress? That was the reason, more than any other, that fashions in general had a skimpy, throwaway appearance. There are other theories about the abrupt and revolutionary change in dress. One is that women were compensating for the loss of their menfolk by adopting a male role. Whatever the reason, the 'boyish woman' was now perfectly in line with the wit and economy of Chanel, the lean, neat clothes of Patou, and the styles of the Brave New World.

Couture detail of an opera cloak, about 1912, by Poiret, bearing the hallmarks of his opulent style: trimmed with a heavy gilt fringe, and with richly brocaded cloth-of-gold sleeves, the square cut cloak has a low waist and is fastened with a huge frog, or gilt braid clasp of fairly pronounced phallic design. The fabric is lined, turquoise satin.

133

Chapter 8

FASHION
GOES STRAIGHT

1920-1930

The 1920s heralded the age of functional fashion, as
opposed to the rather *Grande Dame* styles of the
previous decades, and the extravagant, theatrical
designs of that great individualist Poiret. His decline
and fall occurred because he was unable to adapt to the
post-war mood and its demand for simplicity. Women
wanted easy-to-wear clothes, and responded to the
tomboy look exemplified by that other great
individualist who practised what she preached —
Coco Chanel.
In contrast to Chanel with her sweaters, her businesslike suits and her costume jewellery, were those
couturiers who designed for the ultra-sophisticated
'Best Dressed' women of international Society —
notably the inveterate gambler and playboy, Jean
Patou, and the urbane, elegant Englishman Edward
Molyneux. These three dominated the
fashions of the decade.
The couturier was now a force to be reckoned with, and
all eyes focused on Paris in the spring and autumn
when the latest designs were paraded in the couture
house collections. It was the heyday of the flapper, with
her short, cropped hair, skimpy skirts and rayon
stockings, her painted nails, and cigarettes that bore
those lipstick traces.

Flapper's foundation — the corselette of 1926 — which disguised natural feminine curves in favour of the flat-chested, waistless style which created the 'boyish' look — the short skirts and cropped hair of the mid Twenties.

'I'll be ready in a minute', fashion drawing by Georges Lepape from the magazine La Gazette du Bon Ton *of 1924–25, shows evening wear by Jeanne Lanvin. Maison Lanvin is still producing couture clothes in the Faubourg St Honoré, having been in business over eighty years.*

Women's dress in the 1920s may be categorized by two basic styles, depending mainly on the height of the hem: the long, tubular, close-fitting dresses of the early Twenties which fell to the ankle; and the short dresses of the mid Twenties with hems just below the knee—the all-time high—where they remained until 1929. Recalling the fashions of those days in her book, *Grace and Favour*, the Duchess of Westminster said, 'Hems went down nearly to the ground in 1923, but were up to the knees by 1925, and the waistline wandered high and low, but throughout the Twenties bosoms and hips were definitely *out*. A lovely figure meant a perfectly straight figure and the slightest suggestion of a curve was scorned as *fat*. The ideal woman's vital statistics would probably have been something like 30–30–30.'

Pleated skirts and two-piece suits with a low belt-line were worn with the little cloche hats introduced by Reboux of Paris. Black, single-strap shoes, worn with light-coloured stockings (now flesh-coloured and in the new artificial silk–rayon) had the effect of making the feet appear rather large, while the cloche hats often had a brim that all but covered the eyes and ears, thus accentuating the nose rather than giving the wearer an air of mystery.

The change had been sudden and startling, and nothing like it had occurred in the history of fashion, except, perhaps, when the neoclassic styles of the early nineteenth century appeared. In 1912 women had worn dresses that made them appear matronly and middle-aged, the ultra-fashionable wearing hobble skirts and swathed in sable wraps with the animals' tails hanging down like a tasseled fringe. Although this mode was a direct heir of Poiret's revolutionary straight-line style, it still owed more to the past than to the future; perhaps the huge hats and floor-length skirts were partly to blame.

Then, within a decade, women had discarded their corsets, cut their hair, and shortened their skirts. With short dresses and silk stockings, lipstick and nail varnish, the Twenties ushered in the age of modern fashions. Light, loose fabrics, pockets, belts and the bob, all were first seen in 1919 and were considered very daring. This was the *garçonne* style that dominated the period, that went with Art Deco and the fashion drawings of Lepape, Drian and Benito, with cocktails and the Charleston. The milestones of that fast-paced decade were the dominance of Patou and Chanel, the American Mainbocher joining French *Vogue*, Lanvin opening a boutique for men, the deaths of Jean-Paul and Gaston Worth, the fall of the house of Poiret, the arrival of Elsa Schiaparelli, and, worth mentioning, the first model agency, Lucy Clayton, founded in 1928.

The most determined step that women took—it amounted to a sacrifice—did not affect the length of their skirts, but the length of their hair. Since a bob was more or less irrevocable, and fashion so horribly quixotic, many women retained their long hair in the early Twenties, but a move towards shorter and neater hairstyles had been evident since 1905—long hair, turned under to look like a bob, was simply a compromise. Hair was now waved by steam perms, and Marcel home perm kits became available: you washed your hair with Amami shampoo ('Friday Night is

"UNE MINUTE, ET JE SUIS PRÊTE..."

ROBE ET MANTEAU DU SOIR, DE JEANNE LANVIN

Bridal gowns by Patou, 1923, when he had definitely arrived and was establishing his future style. Patou's approach was towards a modern, clean and streamlined look, a geometric elegance. His clothes were nevertheless designed to please men since, according to Patou, women 'adorn themselves in view of masculine admiration'.

Amami Night', went the slogan) and fixed it with a Marcel perm. Wigs, or 'transformations' as they were called, were handy making it much easier to present an up-to-date *coiffure* as they could be worn over long hair.

The boyish look — Styles of emancipation

In 1923 the bob finally arrived. Hairdressers kept bottles of smelling salts handy, to revive those clients who swooned at seeing the shorn locks of their crowning glory fall to the floor. The bob was a short, masculine style which had originated in New York (some say invented by Irene Castle) and had many versions, straight or waved — the Charleston, the Egyptian, the Paloma, the French, and, by 1927, the rather severe Eton crop or shingle, known in America as the 'boyish bob' and in France as the *garçon*. Some brave souls resisted the trend. Mary Pickford held out until 1927 when her long locks were finally sacrificed to fashion. Her audience, it is said, never forgave her.

The woman of the age was described by Celia Cole in the magazine *Delineator* as having 'a darling little head on top of a slender, supple body not at all concealed by its extremely simple frock—that is she! Far more like a boy than a woman.' It may seem as if emancipation had reached the stage of defeminization, with women adopting male roles in what was seen, then, as a permissive society in which cherished traditions were being flaunted. In Britain, women had won the vote in 1918, and by 1923 a woman had been elected Chairman of the Trades Union Congress. Women were allowed ·(with much resistance) into Oxford University in 1920, although Cambridge stood firm, and in 1921 a jury elected, for the first time, a woman foreman, and a woman was called to the bar.

The boyish look symbolizes Twenties fashions, but it by no means appealed to everyone. Older women retained 'sensible' styles and did not venture into the future. The young women were simply enjoying their new-found physical freedom and sharing the pleasures of vigorous indoor and outdoor pursuits, in response to the *zeitgeist*. Active young women could affect the sporty look by donning a bandeau as worn then (and now) by tennis pros, or the no-nonsense berets and brogues of the golfing set; miniature golf was all the rage in New York (there were 150 penthouse putting greens in Manhattan in 1926). When on vacation, the new woman could now reveal areas of white flesh unaccustomed to daylight in her one-piece bathing suit. Bathers paid a sort of lip-service to propriety by wearing stockings to the knee, which may have had an unintentionally erotic effect.

For a brief spell in 1923 fashion fell again under the influence of the antique when the craze for Egyptian designs followed the discovery by Howard Carter of Tutankhamun's tomb. This was the signal for fashion designers and manufacturers to overreach themselves and flood the market with oriental fabrics and scarab jewellery. Marginally more restrained, the couturiers produced romantic costumes, notably Molyneux's born-again Pharaoh design, as worn by his top model Sumurun (ex-Lucile) bearing a spray of gladioli and flanked by two 'slave' children, the whole owing more to Poiret than to 'King Tut'. By a lucky coincidence, an 'Egyptian' horse—Papyrus—won the 1923 Derby. 'There was scarcely any aspect of female dress and adornment which was not touched at some point during the 1920s by the vogue,' said Barbara Baines of this Egyptian renaissance in her book *Fashion Revivals*. It was matched by a craze for the Chinese game of mah-jongg which swept America in 1922 and promoted the sale of Chinese robes and fans as well as joss sticks.

In spite of the popularity of kimono-cut dresses trimmed with fashionable monkey fur, the voice of America was making itself heard loud and clear: bandleader Paul Whiteman was a superstar, and tea dances were all the rage; jazz was king, and 77 million people went to the cinema every week. Seventh Avenue was the main consumer, and the Rue de la Paix the principle producer, of fashions.

All the Beautiful People—Personal embodiment of the times

The fashion-conscious woman in America, Britain and France could read *Vogue, Harper's Bazaar, La Gazette du Bon Ton* and *Jardin des Modes*—and in Germany, the new, glossy fashion

'La Douce Nuit', *1920, drawing by André Marty for* La Gazette du Bon Ton *of a design from Maison Worth. The dress was probably created by Jean-Philippe Worth, who specialized in evening wear. Maison Worth holds the record as the longest surviving couture house, from 1860 until its take-over by Paquin in 1954. Paquin, the second oldest house, closed down in 1956.*

magazine *Die Dame* — magazines that would tell her all she needed to know, and more. If they failed her, she could turn to the wonderful *Vanity Fair*, America's culture magazine *par excellence*. All the Beautiful People featured in the pages of the *Fair* — the Astors, the Castles, the Astaires, the Barrymores, Gertrude Lawrence, Tallulah Bankhead, Maxine Elliott and Isadora Duncan. Watchful of priorities and gauging their readers' tastes, the *Fair*, under its legendary editor Frank Crowninshield, did profiles of Beau Brummell and Rudolph Valentino, and a cartoon of the psychoanalyst Sigmund Freud.

And what they wore — with the exception of Freud — was eagerly noted. A feature on the tennis star Suzanne Lenglen reports that she wore 'a white silk dress that barely flutters below the knees. White silk stockings with white shoes. Above this background of white, hair as black as a raven's wing bound with a brilliant orange band. Perfectly moulded arms, bare and brown from many suns — the entire effect being one of extreme vividness — an effect immediately to catch and hold the eye.'

Suzanne Lenglen was well equipped to endorse fashions because she was, of course, French, and moreover she was dressed by Jean Patou. Following her appearance on the courts at St Cloud outside Paris, in 1921, there was a rush to buy orange bandeaux. Her fans should have waited, for the next day Lenglen appeared wearing a band of crimson, and the day after, a band of green . . . Patou designed clothes for her both on and off the court, as he did for American tennis champion Helen Wills. It would seem that Lenglen was the personal embodiment of the *zeitgeist*. Fashion journalist Meredith Etherington-Smith makes a bold claim for Lenglen and Patou (in her book *Patou*) when she says, 'Suzanne Lenglen summed up the essence of athletic youth, competitiveness and vigour. Her plain, light colours and practical clothes transmitted this subconscious idea perfectly, and her sports clothes were to influence every facet of fashion design for nearly a decade.'

Patou had immaculate taste, a sure and almost severe eye for design, and masterly tailoring. Yet, like many couturiers of the Twenties and Thirties he is remembered by the general public more for his perfume, Joy, than for his couture styles, just as Chanel is known for Chanel No. 5, Lanvin for Arpège, Rochas for Femme, and Dior for Miss Dior; perfume, always a steady source of revenue, continued long after the house styles had passed into fashion history.

The couturiers who exerted the greatest influence on the Twenties were Chanel, Patou, Vionnet and Lanvin. Jeanne Lanvin was the most senior, having been born in 1867, with Vionnet following in 1876. Patou, born in 1880, was older than Chanel by three years and the two were arch-rivals, Chanel impatient and 'radiating intolerance', Patou, disdainful, calculating, fastidious. The late, great fashion journalist Ernestine Carter remembered Chanel as 'jealous, petty, shrewd and suspicious. She fought with everyone.' She set her sights on Patou, Jacques Heim (who had introduced Chanel to the use of rabbit fur), Antonio del Castillo and her most hated rival, Schiaparelli — 'that Italian artist who makes dresses' and whom Chanel reputedly tried to set on fire!

Patou bathing suits were sold in his beachwear shop in Deauville from 1924. They were the first beach garments to be designed by a couturier, and some bore the JP monogram — another couture innovation. Patou made his name from the elegance and chic of his sportswear, an area of couture barely exploited in the early Twenties, and it was sporting clothes that, to a large extent, influenced the designs of fashions, with their new-found freedom of movement.

To Mrs Carter, Chanel was 'still a Fashion Immortal'. One of the problems was that Chanel and Patou had similar aims. 'Just as Patou dressed the elegant, intelligent woman to appeal to men, so did Chanel,' says Meredith Etherington-Smith. 'Both of them were working to the same end: to abolish frills, to make clothes that were easy to wear, that didn't swamp the personality. Their design language was similar. Chanel's was more sinuous, Patou's more architectural.' Conflict and couture go hand-in-hand, to the accompaniment of back-biting, the snapping of scissors, the stamping of feet, and innuendoes as subtle as sackcloth. Such was the enmity between Chanel and Patou that neither *Vogue* nor *Harper's Bazaar* would risk featuring them on facing pages.

Gabrielle Chanel, in her garden in 1929. Chanel's clothes and her costume jewellery were ideally suited to a society in a hurry. Where that society thought it was going is debatable, but the mood of the times reflected Chanel's own independence. Whereas previously styles of dress had evolved slowly, ideas now 'caught on' fast.

141

A three-piece dress, embroidered with steel thread, by Doeuillet, in 1923, and a red velvet coat, drawn for the magazine Art-Goût-Beauté. The House of Doeuillet was founded in 1900 by a designer from Callot Soeurs, in the Place Vendôme. The House merged with Doucet in 1928, thereafter producing designs under the Doeuillet-Doucet label.

It is more than likely that some fashion styles were created solely for the purpose of scoring points: when Chanel raised her hems, Patou responded by lowering his; Chanel timed the opening of her collection to coincide with that of her rival's. The chic, gamin Anita Loos, who wrote *Gentlemen Prefer Blonds* (Anita was a brunette) and dressed at Chanel *and* Patou (which must have taken courage), said of Patou that he 'made Chanel look like a milliner. He revolutionized the way women dress. Before him it was all ruffles and flounces and after it was clean and elegant. Chanel was nowhere, compared with him.'

Patou and the 'New Style'

Patou came from a comfortable, bourgeois background. His family were tanners, but he himself became first a furrier, then a dressmaker and finally, in 1911, a tailor, so he had a solid grounding for couture. Indeed, such was the quality of his workmanship that his clothes, like those of Chanel, wore well even after being well worn. His style was of rigorous simplicity and neatness, and a clean-lined, almost geometric elegance. It was very much in the Cubist, Art Deco manner of symmetrical design broken by oblique seams; the style was very pervasive in the Twenties, when even patisserie was decorated in what was called the 'New Style'. Patou used Cubist motifs on bathing costumes, on beautifully tailored day dresses, sweaters, blouses, skirts and jackets, some bearing, as part of the intrinsic design, his monogram, JP.

In his immaculate, dark suits, spats and grey Homburg hat, Patou was the acme of masculine elegance, a playboy *par excellence* and according to his close friend and associate, the Society columnist Elsa Maxwell, a passionate gambler. 'It is safe to say that Patou wagered and lost more money in the casinos of France and Monte Carlo than any other gambler in history.' He combined lavish spending with a shrewd business sense and by 1926 had an annual turnover, in today's equivalent, of £5,000,000. Several couturiers adopted the life-style of the society they dressed—for one thing it was sound public relations to see and be seen in Biarritz, Deauville, Cannes and Monte Carlo.

Poiret had shown how it should be done, with his beige-coloured Torpedo Renault and matching chauffeur. Patou owned Hispano-Suiza sports cars, and so did Molyneux, but if they raced each other down the Rue de Rivoli it isn't recorded.

The impeccable Patou (note the two-tone 'co-respondent' shoes), about 1925. The location is probably Deauville, where the smart set went for a fashionable suntan.

The American mannequin Lillian Farley, who modelled as Dinarzade, remembers those unrepeatable, far-off days in her memoirs: 'A Hispano-Suiza was sent to fetch us . . . A footman opened the door and led us upstairs to a dressing room. Palatial was the word for this. The walls were inlaid with minute squares of gold mosaic . . . a dozen heavy crystal and gold perfume bottles, graduating in size, stood on the dressing table. In the hall, Patou's butler was shaking cocktails, and the others were already in the library talking to Madame Lucile.' This was not Lucile, Lady Duff Gordon, but Patou's *premier*, the top-ranking dressmaker in a couture house who translates a couturier's ideas into reality.

'Once it's cut, it's cut' — How couturiers work

Couturiers have their own individual ways of preparing for a collection and designing the variety of garments that they intend to show. Chanel, for example, designed empirically 'as she went along. She never prepared sketches in advance, but worked with pins in her mouth, scissors on a tape around her neck, cutting and pinning on the ever-patient mannequins. Claude Baillén watched her in action, "Keep working till you hate the sight of it." Unerringly she undid seams, stripped off mistakes fold by fold, girdled a dress round her like a rampart. "The underarm is never big enough, and once it's cut, it's cut." The cutters watched nervously as she cut and pruned. "Such stinginess, you can't move that sleeve — anyone would think that the object was to be uncomfortable!" '

By contrast, Patou planned well in advance, preparing meticulous sketches which were then translated into the *toiles* — the unbleached calico patterns cut on the dressmaker's stand or on the house mannequin. The *toiles* give you the pattern for the dress, which is then made up in a suitable fabric. But first, the fabric may be hung on the mannequin to see how it falls, and forms folds and drapes. Embroideries, trimmings, buttons, accessories, would each have been chosen in advance and in sympathy with the character of the fabric.

Since in those days couturiers designed with a specific client or clients in mind, the mannequin would be chosen who best represented the client's physique and perhaps her style. The couturier, working with the *premier*, laid out the design in the selected fabric. Fabrics were chosen with great deliberation, and most couturiers had cloth specially designed and woven for them. A house such as Rodier, or Bianchini-Ferier in Lyon, designed fabrics commissioned by such couturiers as Maggy Rouff, Poiret, Worth, Lanvin, et al.

Jean Patou's styles have now come the full circle. They could easily be worn today, and, indeed, Patou's own philosophy of fashion suits our way of life very well. 'Fashion', he said, 'is a living thing and, in consequence, evolves from day to day, from hour to hour, and from minute to minute.'

Anita Loos' observation that Patou made Chanel 'look like a milliner' hardly does justice to one whom many fashion commentators regard as the greatest couturier ever. If Patou mirrors the ideals of today, so does Chanel. She bought flair and style out of the couture house and into the street as no other couturier has

Mlle Nikitina modelling a Chanel suit in 1929, photographed by Seeberger. The suit is quilted velvet with a lining that matches the blouse. The net fringed hat or bonnet is by Le Monnier.

Chanel with Lady Iya Abdy in 1929. Iya Abdy was over six feet tall and was given to wearing huge felt hats. The daughter of a Russian actor and herself an actress, she appeared in Cocteau's Oedipus Rex, *for which Chanel designed eccentric costumes. Chanel's ex-model Toto Koopman told Brigid Keenan, 'She was quite extraordinary, like a giant blond Garbo. She wore very simple clothes but always chose odd hats. She was a tremendous friend of Chanel who dressed her for nothing because she looked so good and knew all the right people.'*

succeeded in doing. Moira Keenan says, 'The secret of the Chanel look was to wear the plainest garment and then pile on to it a mass of costume jewellery (you could use the real stuff she said, so long as it was so extravagant it looked like junk) along with other well-thought-out accessories which gave the outfit richness and glamour without altering its basic simplicity. Chanel taught us the lesson we dress by today: that the clothes themselves are less important than what you put with them and how you wear them. It was she who invented what fashion editors are fond of calling the "Total Look".'

The Total Look was worn by millions of women when Chanel made her famous come-back in the early 1950s, the 'Chanel suit' being copied by such retail manufacturers as Wallis in London. It seemed, then, that every woman was wearing an oatmeal jacket and skirt, or cardigan suit, the top with its braided edging, the hem weighted down with a discreetly hidden gold chain, the silk lining matching the blouse—it was the only 'uniform' couture has ever produced. It seemed a small step from her early years as a couturier, when, as *Vogue* commented, 'Her simple chiffon dresses with their petal skirts, deep-cut backs and low sashes were worn by smart women around the world.'

Chanel No. 5 — The sweet smell of success

Inspired perhaps by the examples of Poiret and Lanvin, she perfected and launched her own scent, the famous Chanel No. 5. It was immortalized by Marilyn Monroe who, when asked what she wore in bed, replied wide-eyed and smiling sweetly, 'Chanel No. 5'. But this story may be apochryphal. Confusion exists, of course, as to the reason why Chanel chose that particular number Some say that it was because the bottle was the fifth one presented to her by the perfumier for her approval, and because 'five is such a pretty number'. Others say that it was because Chanel's birthday fell on the fifth and that she always launched her collections on the fifth, which doesn't tally with the claim that Chanel launched her collections to coincide with those of her rivals, and her birthday in fact was on the nineteenth.

Anyway, she packaged her scent in a throw-away bottle, the contents of which endowed the wearer with the smell of 'sandlewood, Russian leather, gardenia and jasmine, Bulgarian roses and magnolia'. This description rather overlooks the fact that Chanel No. 5 was the first of the 'modern' perfumes, with an entirely chemical, or aldehyde (an organic compound based on ethyl alcohol), base. Although synthetic, the moderns can recreate the scents of certain flowers that do not yield the oil needed for making perfumes, or 'fragrances' as they are called today. Chanel No. 5 is in the same stable — if you will forgive the phrase — as Lanvin's Arpège; Rochas's Madame Rochas; Givenchy's L'Interdit; Worth's Je Reviens and Yves Saint Laurent's Rive Gauche.

Chanel's great perfume is chic, sophisticated and frank — rather like its creator — and it was a tremendous success. Her premises in the Rue Cambon expanded to take in five extra buildings, providing working space for the three thousand workers in her employ. By 1930 it is said that she was paying over 17 million francs a year in taxes! No wonder that *haute couture* was the number two of French exports. And number one? I don't know, but it was probably wine.

In common with most couturiers, Chanel had good business sense. 'We are in trade, not art,' she maintained, although she displayed the perfectionism and single-minded dedication shared by many artists. She would take a suit to pieces 25 times, reducing everything to its simplest and most practical elements. 'A suit only looks good when the woman who wears it seems to have nothing on underneath,' she declared firmly, a view which might have ruled out most of her clientele and potential custom.

Her suits had pockets that were meant to contain things, and she taught that there should never be a button without a buttonhole. But her output was by no means confined to the suit with the sensible pockets. She designed dresses and evening wear, wonderfully restrained designs of muted colours, or black contrasting with a single, strong colour, clothes of the kind that prompted admiration from Balenciaga, himself the master of restraint and monochromatic invention. Hervé Mille said of Chanel

The most famous perfume in the world. Chanel launched Numero 5 *in 1920. It was created by chemist Ernest Beaux and reputedly contains 128 ingredients (some say eighty), and it is this perfume that forms the basis of Chanel's fortune — said to be about 15 million dollars at her death. Indeed, perfumes and accessories are the mainstay of most couture houses.*

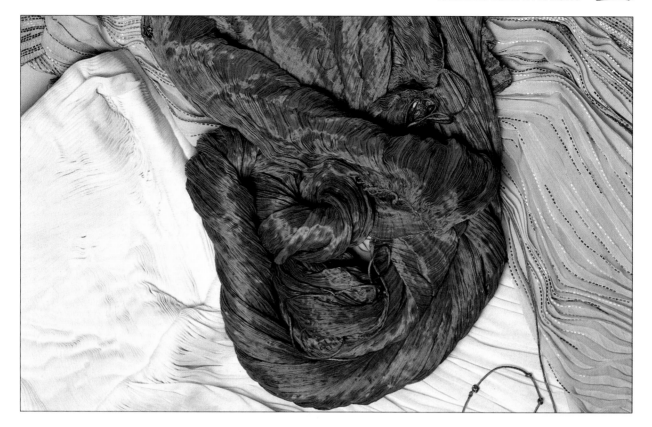

that she was not a fashion but a *style*. Fashion becomes *démodé*, but style never.

She, and the other couturiers of the 1920s—those that harnessed the spontaneous, random energy of fashion and directed its course—seem to have halted the recurring cycle of fashion, as documented by Agnes Young. The tubular cycle, which arrived more or less on time in the late 1890s, is still going strong today, despite a brief spell of flaring skirts in 1918 (though Lanvin continued to show them through the Twenties) and Dior's New Look of 1947, and it seems likely to remain. It has thus overstayed its natural leave by 45 years.

Couture details: Pleated fabrics, TOP LEFT, by Grès, in extraordinarily fine, hand-stitched pleats in a classic design that is unmistakably and inimitably Grès. In the CENTRE the equally inimitable process of pleating by Marinaro Fortuny (see page 128) and BELOW, pleats with beading on an evening dress by Patou.

One of the reasons for this may be the dominance of Vionnet's bias cut which favoured the long, lean, hugging and clinging styles, and also the classic, draped dresses of Madame Grés. Whether in deference to the cycle (a phenomenon unknown or ignored by the couturiers, and to most fashion historians at the time) or in response to one of the other mysterious dynamic forces of fashion, a few couturiers did introduce the awaited bell cycle, notably Molyneux and Balenciaga, at the outbreak of World War II. But in the 1920s, fashion was still on the threshold of a great adventure. Why, women didn't use nail varnish until 1926! Patou, mindful of his American clients, took the unprecedented step of sailing to New York to recruit six mannequins for his Paris shows. One of the girls was Edwina Prue, a blond, fresh-faced 'typical American girl' as Patou described her, and, as she described herself, 'American girls were so neat and clean-looking in those days. I suppose we were very attractive. We wore pleated skirts and little sweaters on which we

Princess Natalie Paley, photographed by Cecil Beaton against a rather suggestive background (bed springs), about 1935. Much taken with her, Beaton described her eyes as star-bright, and said that 'her laughter tinkles like a mountain stream over pebbles'.

sewed white piqué collars and cuffs. We buffed our fingernails and put Vaseline on our eyelids and wore pink silk stockings with black patent pumps.'

American clients now attended the Paris collections to watch American mannequins, and an American, Main Rousseau Bocher, had even become the fashion editor of French *Vogue*— though at least his name was partly French. But the French did not entirely dominate the couture scene. Maggy Rouff was Belgian, Robert Piguet was Swiss, and Edward Molyneux was English— with a touch of Irish and Hungarian. The Captain had returned from the War minus one eye, but with an MC, so he was not lacking in courage to 'storm the citadel of fashion', as he put it. During the Twenties he was feeling his way and forming his own personal style. Partnered by the indomitable Elsa Maxwell, 'the hostess with the mostest', Molyneux opened a night club, *Le Jardin de Ma Soeur*, so as to gain prestige among the smart set and thereby attract potential custom to his couture house.

Molyneux began his career working in London for Lucile, with whom he got a job having won a newspaper competition for dress design. His undoubted flair marked him out as a potential couturier, and Lucile sent Molyneux to manage her Paris office. He opened his own house in 1919, and for a while showed the influence of Lucile's romantic, theatrical style exemplified in a cloak he designed for one of the Dolly Sisters, the hugely successful music hall act of the Twenties. Jenny Dolly's cloak was of white chiffon, 18 feet long covered with white feathers and five thousand real gardenias. It was far removed from the style for which Molyneux eventually became known—tailored suits and pleated skirts, understated elegance and simplicity.

Vionnet—'A genius with the scissors'

In 1926, when skirts were undecided whether to go up or down, Madeleine Vionnet introduced her bias cut. There had been a curious sort of compromise whereby dresses, especially evening gowns, had a narrow train of chiffon or some other material matching the dress fabric, which was attached to the hip and either trailed on the floor or hung just to the ankle. This was followed by the 'handkerchief drape'. This style, especially suited to evening dresses, is attributed to Vionnet, who was described by American *Vogue* as 'an artist in fabric, as Picasso is in paint'. Norah Waugh explained, 'Handkerchief drapes are so called because they originated in the use of rectangular pieces of material such as a handkerchief square. One right angle was attached to the skirt, the corner usually being cut off and the rest of the material hanging free in folds, making a zig-zag edge.'

Cecil Beaton considered Vionnet 'a genius with her scissors. She changed fashion.' Her bias cut was a major contribution to fashion dressmaking techniques, as previously described (page 123), and as Ernestine Carter tells us, Vionnet expoited all its permutations: for entire dresses, for lozenge-shaped or triangular insets, for bias-cut petals, handkerchief points and long panels, making 'dresses that seem to float over the body, suggesting without revealing'.

If hemlines showed some ambiguity, men's fashion took an assertive step when students at Oxford University introduced 'Oxford bags' (claimed by some to have originated in Cambridge), the ultra-wide trousers that measured a good 24 inches around each leg. They soon reached America, followed by the fashion for 'plus-fours', or knickerbockers that ended just below the knee. Americans were spared the Men's Dress Reform Movement, however, founded by the psychologist J. C. Flugel. Dress Reform dances were held in London, where members with more courage than dress sense attired themselves in short-sleeved tunics with a wavy hem, belted at the waist, short trousers to the knee, and white cotton socks.

In spite of this, London was still the centre of menswear, and whatever an English gentleman wore was eventually copied or adapted by everyone else. *Vanity Fair*'s editor, Frank Crownin-shield, was once asked by *Vogue* editor Edna Woolman Chase if he would care to carry a feature on 'The Well-Dressed Man'. Crowninshield refused. 'But darling,' he said, 'a gentleman *knows* how to dress.' In America, the blazer, white flannels and white shoes could be worn for the popular pastime of tea dancing. Strictly speaking, and mens' fashions were indeed strict, any shoes other than black leather were regarded with suspicion. Even the Prince of Wales—and he was passionately interested in clothes —was not above censure when he appeared wearing suede shoes, prompting the editor of the austere *The Tailor & Cutter* to say, 'I was brought up to think that suede shoes were only worn in private by consenting adults.'

Oxford bags and plus-fours. There were also 'plus-twos', a slim-fitting style of riding breeches. Plus-fours that hung a good four inches below the knee were particularly smart.

149

Dress manufacturer's sketches for a trade pattern book, ABOVE and OPPOSITE. The above model, Orphée, has a fur-trimmed skirt, collar and cuffs, and is an example of the very fashionable afternoon coat of the year 1928.

Two-tone Oxford shoes, later to become known as 'co-respondent' shoes, could be worn by women, but only by men if they smuggled them out of the country and wore them on the Riviera. Brown shoes were just permissible, though, as informal wear. Two-tone shoes with a strap or 'bar' had been popularized by Chanel and were an intrinsic part of her ensemble. Here, again, she was a leader in that couturiers ignored accessories until Chanel used matching elements to make a cohesive whole.

'It' — Couture goes to Hollywood

What clearly had an effect on fashions, apart from Chanel's Functional Chic, were the stars of the silent screen. From the earliest days of the movies, film producers had relied on Paris couture to dress the stars glamorously, influencing the tastes of that generation, and others to follow. Writing in the Thirties, in his essay, *The Road to Wigan Pier*, George Orwell observed that the years of the Depression had actually promoted the consumption of cheap luxuries, especially clothes, and going to the movies. 'You may have three halfpence in your pocket', wrote Orwell, 'and not a prospect in the world; but in your new clothes you can stand on the street corner, indulging in a private daydream of yourself as Clark Gable or Greta Garbo, which compensates you for a great deal.'

Couture fashions, disseminated as copies in the department stores, by mail order, and advertised in the press to an eager public, were now endorsed through the medium of cinema. By the late 1920s well over a hundred million people went to the cinema every week in America, and what movie stars wore could and did inspire millions of women. Even the stars' informal, off-the-set wear inspired 'flash fashions' for such things as Garbo-style slouch hats and berets. Writing *A History of the Cinema*, author Eric Rhode said, 'Hollywood couturiers had the difficult task of anticipating public taste (often by years) as well as creating clothes that would look exciting with flamboyant sets.'

Star clients for the couture houses were immensely prestigious. Poiret dressed Valentino's wife, Rambova, while Patou was a particular favourite and dressed Mary Pickford ('America's Sweetheart'), Louise Brooks, Pola Negri and the legendary Gloria Swanson, who also dressed at Lucien Lelong. Lucile's younger sister, Elinor Glyn, followed her romantic shockers with a novel, simply titled *It*, and was invited to Hollywood in 1928.

In the 1920s a company such as Paramount needed to produce over a hundred films a year to stay in business and supply their circuits. By the mid Twenties they had run out of stories, and producer Jesse Lasky imported a contingent of writers from Europe, including Maurice Maeterlinck the Belgian dramatist, Somerset Maugham and Elinor Glyn — a somewhat disparate group. Sam Goldwyn had great hopes for Elinor. 'Her name', he said, 'is synonymous with the discovery of sex appeal in the cinema.'

Miss Glyn was asked to select the girl who best represented the 'It' quality, in other words, sex appeal — and she chose a vivacious redhead from Brooklyn called Clara Bow. Clara wasn't too sure what 'It' meant, but she gave of her best which proved more than sufficient. *Vanity Fair* called her 'the orchidaceous Clara, the super-flapper of them all—the hyper-reality and extra-ideality of a million or more film-goers . . . the genus American girl, refined, washed, manicured, permanent-waved and exalted herewith.'

Movie moguls, Cecil B. DeMille in particular, took painstaking care over fashions in dress, jewellery, hairstyling and, of course, make-up. This was certainly the first fashion influence exerted by the flickering, silent, black-and-white era, featuring such stars as Theda Bara, Pola Negri, Mary Pickford and the Gish sisters. Theda Bara, known as 'The Vamp' had introduced a dramatic style of make-up for the eyes, using mascara, that gave her the requisite smouldering look of the *femme fatale*. The creator of this face was a Polish make-up artist from the Moscow State Theatre, who had arrived in Hollywood in 1914—Max Factor.

Patou's bombshell and Wall Street's crash

Endorsement by the movies helped to promote the wider use of make-up, previously commended in advertisements by Sarah Bernhardt with her Bernhardt Beauty Bath, and the French actress Gaby Deslys with her cosmetic Le Secret. Now that Max Factor, with his first cosmetic product, Supreme Greasepaint, had shown that romantic stars like Mary Pickford wore make-up, it became more universally acceptable. Hitherto it had been of somewhat dubious respectability. Women applied rouge very discreetly until the liberal use of cosmetics was countenanced after the War.

Richard Corson, author of *Fashions in Make-up* says, 'Perhaps for the first time since the Ancient Egyptians, the unlimited use of cosmetics came to be universally accepted, both socially and morally.' The moral issue had been acknowledged and make-up sanctioned by the editor of American *Vogue* in 1920. 'Even the most conservative and prejudiced people now concede that a woman exquisitely made up may yet be, in spite of seeming frivolity, a faithful wife and a devoted mother.'

Make-up, as Corson points out, also had the psychological benefit of emphasizing youth and longevity. One can usually find evidence of a coming change a decade or more before the change becomes apparent. Thus, in America, face powder and the powder-puff, slide-tube lipsticks, eyebrow pencils, rouge, face cream, and even beauty spots, were on sale in 1915. By 1921 there were many beauty parlours throughout Europe and America, and the producers, notably Helena Rubinstein, Elizabeth Arden and Yardley, were well established.

The rouged cheeks, painted lips and the powdered nose were part of the flapper style, and when skirts reached the knee in the late 1920s, girls felt obliged to powder their knees too. It was to be a short-lived fad. In his winter collection of 1929, Jean Patou did something that filled his order books, delighted his clients, enraged Chanel, infuriated Hollywood producers, and made dress manufacturers' stock obsolete overnight. He dropped the hemline to mid calf. Almost as though in sympathy, or by pre-arrangement, the Wall Street Stock Market fell, and with a crash that reverberated around the world. The two events are not thought to be connected, but it was bad news for Parisian couture.

Jeu de Roi *jacket and skirt with the unresolved hemline, just before skirts dropped yet again. 1928 was a year of little dresses with pleats, a low belt, cloche hat and handbag.*

151

Chapter 9

SHOCKS AND SHARES

1930-1940

The Thirties started off badly, with the Depression affecting most of the fashion industry, although the couture houses managed to survive and weather the storm. It was, in some respects, the perfect climate for a survivor and innovator like Elsa Schiaparelli, whose 'elegant outrage' and 'Shocking' perfume delighted and scandalized the fashionable world.

When compared with the romantic style of Lanvin, the classic designs of Alix and Vionnet, the restrained elegance of Molyneux and with Mainbocher, 'Schiap's' approach was pure show business. Nevertheless, her 'toy soldier' look, with its wide shoulders and slim waist was to remain the major trend in fashions through the decade and into the World War II. If there was one manifestation of the period that was compatible with Elsa's style, it was Hollywood and the movies, which captured, and influenced, an audience of millions.

Paris summer outfit for 1931. Blouse with bolero jacket and matching skirt in blue marocain. In 1930 the waistline, previously at hip level, returned to normal, and skirt hems dropped. In 1931 skirts continued their downward trend, and Vogue *was reporting a wider shoulder and narrower waist. The general effect, for most of the decade, was to emphasize height and impossibly slim hips.*

Only the most eminent and powerful couturiers wield enough influence to create a major fashion change such as Patou achieved with his dropped hems. Chanel could have done it, lowering the hems on her little black dresses and pleated skirts, but Patou thought of it first and had the courage to make it one of the main features of his collection in 1929. It may seem to us today hardly anything to write home about, but short of bringing back the bustle (which was to occur in 1934) there were no other options—a miniskirt would have been the ultimate horror to the fastidious Patou.

A characteristic of 1930s' fashions was the almost total absence of hips, and a gradual widening of the shoulders through the latter part of the decade. If couture fashion can be accepted as an art form, then we might refer to the Thirties as the Tubist period, reflecting the current styles in painting and graphics for dynamism and the aesthetics of utility. The ideal was established through fashion drawings, in particular the covers of *Vogue* magazine, in dress catalogues, and by a handful of bean-pole models carefully photographed to emphasize the cylindrical style.

For the 'average fashionable woman' a slim figure was achieved by dieting and by recourse to sheath corselettes, foundation garments by such manufacturers as Gossard and Berlei, made in satin and handknit elastic (Lastex) boned at the back and over the diaphragm, and with a firm lace top in place of a brassière. The long, lean look gave women a lissom elegance very well suited to inexpensive materials such as wool and rayon mixtures, linen, linen and cotton or tweed mixtures, georgette and crêpe de Chine.

Hats were generally small, close fitting and worn at an angle, though there was a brief period for coolie hats and tricorne hats in 1934. Day dresses went through a period in 1932 when many had yoked bodices or skirts, with gores and godets, and designs included asymmetrical seams: for two or three years, Cubism flirted with Tubism. By 1935, yokes had gone, dresses were even longer, and belts and big buttons were the thing. Unfortunately, shoe designs lagged behind fashions, and the clumsy one-strap court shoe gave the feet a rather institutional appearance.

Fashion cycles do not outwardly reflect major economic events, for better or for worse, and looking at the fashions of 1930 there is no indication that the economy was suffering the greatest depression in modern history. In France, following the Wall Street Crash of 1929, ten thousand employees were made redundant, and the jobs of half a million were threatened throughout the fashion industry, which included the suppliers to couture —fabric manufacturers, dyers and weavers, button makers, and so on. As an export item couture fell from second to twenty-seventh place. American buyers cancelled their orders, and couturiers in France suffered severe withdrawal symptoms at the sudden lack of dollars.

Yet even during periods of economic depression there are always people with money to spend on luxuries—and for some, clothes are a priority. Arthur Schlesinger, writing in 1957 in *The Age of Roosevelt*, said that by 1929 the combined savings of the 60,000 families in America with the highest incomes were almost as much as those of the bottom 25 million. 'The mass of the population lacked the necessary increase in purchasing power to enable them to absorb the increase in goods.' But not the top echelon of society. Even supposing a good proportion of those 60,000 families suffered from the Stock Market Crash, there remained those with sufficient wealth to weather the storm and continue to support the couturiers.

The Best Dressed List—The women who were fashion

Couture houses survived by cut-backs and staff reductions, by getting credit from textile manufacturers and using capital accrued during the rich years of the Twenties, and because of the faithful patronage of the 'Best Dressed List'. This list was, to borrow a phrase of Ernestine Carter's, a 'tongue-in-the-chic' poll, taken by the leading couturiers in the Twenties, to decide which of their distinguished clients were the most elegant. Said *The New York Times*, 'A candidate must do more than invest the sum of $50,000 with the Paris dressmaking trade. She must have brains, poise and vivacity.' Fashion journalist Brigid Keenan, writing in 1977 in *The Women We Wanted To Look Like*, said that couturiers in those days designed for 'a handful of rich Society women who rivalled each other in smartness, snobbery and wealth. These women *were* fashion. Every bow or bead they wore was reported in the papers, and the loveliest among them were in constant demand as the subjects for glossy magazine photographs.'

These were the women, the leaders of Society in the post-war years, who inspired and gave impetus to the creativity of the couturiers. They were not merely elegant and wealthy, but celebrated beauties. The Princess Natalie Paley, who according to Cecil Beaton was 'the most significant beauty after Garbo', was the daughter of the Grand Duke Paul, a Russian exile in Paris. The photographer Hoyningen-Huene featured her in *Vanity Fair*, as 'The Most Beautiful Woman I ever photographed'. Beaton probably would have chosen her too, but Huene had the first choice, so Beaton selected the American Mona Harrison Williams, a woman of exceptional poise and finely detailed elegance.

Natalie Paley married the couturier Lucien Lelong—there's a photograph of her delicate and poignant features in 1928, dressed by her husband in a low-waisted, pleated, beige crêpe dress and a long coat of grey wool trimmed on the collar and cuffs with fox fur. As 'The Prettiest Woman in Paris' she had much close competition: the American oil heiress Millicent Rogers, for example, or Mrs Dudley Ward, who was tiny, boyish and with baby-blue eyes.

The couturiers, choosing contenders for the Best Dressed List, would hardly dare place its members in order of supremacy, not with eyeball-to-eyeball rivals such as the Ladies Colefax and Cunard, or influential hostesses such as Madame Martine de Hoz, the Duchesse de Gramont, the Vicomtesse de Noailles, and Lady Mendl. And certainly not if they were to include, as they must, Mrs Reginald 'Daisy' Fellowes, the granddaughter of Isaac Singer. The Depression made hardly a dent in the sewing machine millions, and Daisy was to become famous, indeed notorious, for her extravagancies, her eccentricity and her perversity. She was

The slimline fashions at the start of the 1930s suited tall women, and the impression of height was emphasized by short, permed hair-styles and small hats that swept back from the forehead. Flounces were a feature that gave a touch of femininity to an otherwise uncompromisingly severe line. Here a tier of four split flounces, or volants, are used on a brown plaid day dress. The collar is white crêpe de Chine, the belt red leather.

dressed by Chanel, but in the early Thirties fanned the flames of emnity by leaving Chanel for Schiaparelli. These, then, were some of the women that sustained Chanel, Patou, Vionnet and Molyneux in their darkest hour. Poiret had closed in 1929, because his collections appeared too extravagant and out of step with the times. In what seemed like a gesture of bravado, Madame Grés actually opened her house in 1930 as Alix, a name she retained until World War II when she changed it to Grés.

The grand style – The fall of Lucile and Poiret

In Britain, when sterling fell to an all-time low in 1931, Lady Houston was still able to put up £100,000 to sponsor the Schneider Trophy air race, in the year when records were being broken on land, sea, on the stock exchange, and in couture. In spite of trade boycotts, Norman Hartnell was attracting American buyers, although Lucile's London house was in decline, and for much the same reason as that of Poiret – she was unable to adapt to the changing styles of dress. This requires, I think, some explanation. Lucile's rich, romantic, theatrical dresses were *démodé* by the mid Twenties. Lucile and Poiret were exponents of the grand style and gesture. They were not lacking in inventiveness but were victims of a fatal egocentricity coupled with extravagance.

Lucile was a top-drawer Court dressmaker, but her personality was unsuited to the vigorous, free, *sportif* mood of the Twenties, that Chanel personified. She was, in short, out of step with the *zeitgeist*; romance had given way to pragmatism. In the fashion business you have to look to the future and it is fatal to be overtaken by events. The fickle nature of fashion is only surpassed by the inconstancy of the clientele.

As for Poiret, he was an artist and turned to landscape painting. Yet even though his couture house was forced to close in 1929 his name held a certain magical attraction: in 1933 the French department store Au Printemps invited Poiret to show four collections a year. He overspent his budget and quit in a huff. In the same year, Liberty's of London asked him to design a collection for their Model Gown Salon. This was more successful, and the fashion writer for *Country Life* applauded the show, recognizing that 'M. Poiret has lost none of his striking originality and individuality.' Poiret had adapted his designs to fall into line with the clinging, bias-cut evening gowns so popular in the Thirties, but alas it was too late.

In 1934, just after *Vanity Fair* had shown a photograph of the celebrated couturier taking breakfast in bed with his wife (he in simple, striped pyjamas, she in an off-the-shoulder nightie), Poiret went on the dole. Impractical and improvident, his was a fine recipe for disaster and, in this respect, he was his own worst enemy. Mindful of his plight and his contribution to couture history, certain members of the organized body of couturiers, the *Chambre Syndicale de la Couture Parisienne*, proposed that Poiret be allotted a subsistence allowance of a thousand francs a month. The proposers were Robert Piguet and Lucien Lelong, backed by Jeanne Lanvin and Madeleine Vionnet. It was then that Poiret learned he was not quite his own worst enemy: it was Jacques

Dresses with yokes, fitted capes or cape collars appeared in 1932. Angular geometric seams were a continued feature of decoration – influenced by the Art Deco and Cubist styles that dominated the world of design.

Copies of two couture summer day dresses of 1931. The one on the right is a Poiret from the catalogue Paris Chic. *In that year Poiret wrote of current fashion designers (and borrowing a famous phrase from Viscount Grey of Falloden), 'They have let the lights go out and they will never be relit.' It was certainly true for this erstwhile* enfant terrible *who was still greatly respected, but out of step with the times. Thirty years later another great couturier, Balenciaga, was to make a similar complaint about the march of progress.*

Worth. Worth vetoed the proposal and ensured that Poiret got nothing. His grandfather, the great Charles Frederick Worth, would probably have turned in his grave.

Chic goes to Hollywood—Couture and the movies

To moderate the grim reality of the Depression, a mood of escapism and forced gaiety prevailed during the early Thirties, and women set a brisk pace in inspired deeds that grabbed world headlines. The ideal, outdoor girl was exemplified by Amelia Earheart. Sporting what may be best described as a 'windblown bob' she was the first woman to pilot the Atlantic alone in 1932.

The Thirties saw a tremendous vogue for evening dresses, in spite of, or perhaps because of, the prevailing Depression—an era of dinner dances and nightingales in Berkeley Square. Evening dresses, almost all of them backless, were available to all as inexpensive ready-to-wear garments from department stores. The wealthy woman, dining at the Ritz, could go to her couturier, for creations such as this gold lamé dress by Vionnet. It appeared in Harper's Bazaar *in 1937, along with the legend: 'The silhouette is young, the* décolletage *is treated most beautifully. This is Vionnet's greatest dress . . . a hush fell when it passed in the Collection . . .' The photograph is by the Surrealist painter and photographer Man Ray, and appeared in the Surrealist Exhibition of 1937, where the dress was mistakenly ascribed to Lucien Lelong.*

The trend of the fashion-conscious aviatrix had already been set by Amy Johnson in 1930 when she flew solo from England to Australia, taking with her a wardrobe of Schiaparelli dresses which probably caused as much comment in Sydney as did her feat of aviation.

In the world of fashion, women more than held their own against the men, with the examples of Grés, Lanvin, Vionnet, Schiaparelli and Chanel. In 1931, *Vanity Fair* nominated Chanel for its 'Hall of Fame' feature, alongside Walt Disney, Daphne du Maurier and Rene Clair. Chanel was chosen because 'she was the first to apply modernism to dressmaking; because she numbers among her friends the most famous men in France; because she combines a shrewd business sense with enormous personal prodigality and a genuine if erratic enthusiasm for the art; and finally because she came to America to make a laudable attempt to introduce chic to Hollywood.'

Sam Goldwyn was the architect of this enterprise, luring Chanel to the celluloid city to dress Gloria Swanson, who was also dressed (in Paris) by Patou and Lelong. Goldwyn had been a glove manufacturer, so he might have had an inkling of the world of couture, and probably chose Chanel because, like Swanson, she was small, elegant and energetic. The film, *Tonight or Never*, was not much of a success; it was to be one of the last of Gloria Swanson's films, and witnessed the debut of Melvyn Douglas as a film star. Chanel's costume designs were too underplayed for Hollywood tastes. 'She made a lady look like a lady', said *The New Yorker* magazine, 'Hollywood wants a lady to look like *two* ladies!'

Designing for the movies is a specialized business and needs a larger-than-life approach combined with an element of fantasy. The movie-goer's desire to escape, once a week, into a make-believe world, sustained the industry throughout the Depression, so that by 1935 there were 39 Hollywood studios. Even if William Powell as the man himself in *The Thin Man* did not inspire a generation of men to sharp dressing and sophisticated wit, a great number of women identified with his partner Myrna Loy, as they did with Jean Harlow, Joan Crawford and Marlene Dietrich. Couturiers were too restrained for designing costumes for the cinema so that the genre had to emerge from the industry independent of, but influenced by, the inventions of couture.

Cecil Beaton, the most informed and influential fashion and social commentator and photographer of the age, was unable to assess Hollywood on any other terms than its own bizarre fantasy world. Joining the daily promenade along Sunset Boulevard he saw starlets 'wearing such clothes as have never even been dreamed of. It is only here that one realizes to what heights the dressmaker's art can soar. Roses, checks, lace, ostrich feathers, chintzes, velvets and furs are put to uses to which we shall never become accustomed, and the shop-windows display attractions of such excruciating taste that one never before realized how dull good taste was, and how lovely bad taste could be.'

Travis Banton, Edith Head, Normal Norell, Gilbert Adrian and Howard Greer were Hollywood's leaders in the field of movie couture, taking styles from Paris or inventing fashions of their own. Schiaparelli was the inspiration behind the broad-shouldered look that Adrian gave Joan Crawford, while Vionnet's designs prompted him to create the silky, slinky dresses worn by the platinum-blond temptress Jean Harlow. Some of the designers had been trained in couture: Howard Greer, who fashioned costumes for Dietrich, had been employed by Lucile, Poiret and Molyneux.

Adrian also trained in Paris and eventually returned to couture in America in 1942, as did Norman Norell, who became, Prudence Glynn claimed, the Balenciaga of America. 'Norell translated the French concept of intrinsic chic into the dream American lifestyle, and offered American women the chance to sample the quality and intransigence of the hautest of *haute couture*.' Combining Hollywood glamour with couture elegance, Norell produced a fabled collection of shimmering, sequined sheath dresses in the 1950s, the ultimate in luxury evening wear.

———✧———

*T*he clothes worn by the stars on screen were usually a season or two—even a year or two—behind Paris fashions, but the clothes they wore off the set gave film designers a source of ideas. Garbo and Crawford were dressed by Schiaparelli, and Gilbert Adrian translated this private persona of fashion into costumes for the screen. When Joan Crawford—with her over-

The backless dress may have evolved, as James Laver suggested, from the swimming costume. By 1935 the halter-neck 'swim-suit' revealed more of the female body than had previously been seen outside the intimacy of the home. The evening dress now took advantage of this 'erogenous zone', while the bias cutting of lightweight fabrics caused dresses to mould to the figure or, as one American (male) observer said appreciatively, to 'cling on tight round the bends'.

Elsa Schiaparelli, whose talent to amuse and to shock made her the most talked about, and imitated, couturier of the Thirties. Photographed by Cecil Beaton in 1937.

applied, dark red, Max Factor lipstick and matching nail varnish, and her rich, dark hair—became 'The Most Imitated Woman in the World', in 1932, other studios persuaded their female stars to dress similarly.

Katherine Hepburn went to Schiaparelli, and throughout the Thirties a bevy of broad-shouldered, immaculately groomed, and somewhat androgynous ladies strode in front of the cameras, culminating in the 1938 epic *The Women* with Norma Shearer, Joan Crawford, Rosalind Russell, Joan Fontaine, and Paulette Goddard heading an all-girl cast—'135 women with men on their minds' went the studio blurb. The men, one imagines, fled in confusion.

Designs were a two-way exchange—if couture was a source of film costumes for lavish musicals and chic comedies, Hollywood also gave impetus to the fashion market. Copies of Adrian's dresses for Crawford reputedly sold by the hundred thousand at Macy's. In Britain the 'Joan Crawford dress' and the 'Ginger Rogers coat' were Marley Gowns' top sellers in the 1930s. But did similar styles reach Au Printemps and Galeries Lafayette, thus coming the full circle?

Together, Hollywood and the couture industry dictated what cosmetics you wore, and how you wore them, aided and abetted by the beauty salons of Elizabeth Arden and Helena Rubinstein. Fashion magazines might well urge subtlety in rouge and lipstick, but they were largely ignored by Schiaparelli, whose lipsticks shades, Shocking, Incarnat, and Pruneau, gave, according to *Harper's Bazaar*, 'the almost indecent allure of Gaugin fruit'. Allure was what women sought, and the cosmetics of allure were up there on the silver screen every Saturday night. Richard Corson, in *Fashions in Make-up*, calculates that ordinary American women bought, in 1938, '52,000 tons of cleansing cream, 18,000 tons of nourishing cream, 27,000 tons of skin lotion, 20,000 tons of complexion soap, and 25,000 tons of rouge, adding up to a total of $400 million' (£162,500,000).

The ritual, previously unknown, of applying lipstick and rouge and of powdering the nose in public became a frequent sight. 'Women who seemed otherwise reasonably well bred', says Corson, 'combed their hair at restaurant tables, left lipstick smears on napkins, towels and glasses, and powdered their noses with dirty, greasy powder puffs from messy vanity cases. The experts advised—pull yourself together before you go out, then leave yourself alone in public.'

Pure Elsa—The shock of Schiaparelli

The 'thoroughly modern', well-dressed city woman of the mid Thirties would wear, out of doors, a hat over her permanent wave, well-defined make-up, a fox fur (preferably silver fox), perhaps a smart two-piece suit with a blouse, a handbag, silk stockings and court shoes. This was the Total Look which varied, of course, according to the season, and was determined by what the fashion magazines decreed. *Vogue*'s fashion scouts sniffed the air, like Borzois, hunting for chic, and they rarely pursued the wrong scents. Quick to perceive new talent, *Vogue* featured in December 1927 a bright Italian star called Elsa Schiaparelli.

In fact, she was a super-nova (her uncle was a noted astronomer), her immediate family being Roman, well-to-do and intellectual, albeit restrictive and stuffy. She was born in Rome, in the Palazzo Corsini, and must have absorbed, throughout her childhood, the Baroque arabesques, curlicues and putti, the sculptural fluidity of Bernini and the *trompe-l'oeil* images in painting. These would later appear as high-relief and highly decorative embroidery in her designs. But this may be a fanciful interpretation of the Schiaparelli extravert style; she may quite simply have identified an area of couture that had not been exploited recently and followed the example of Poiret, who became a friend and confidant and knew the value of shock tactics.

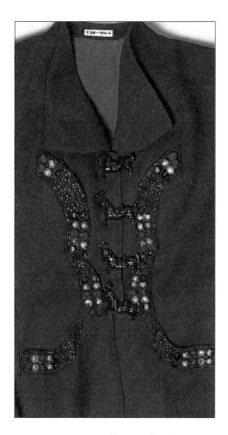

Schiaparelli was the first couturier to use zip fasteners, and the first to introduce novelty buttons, or 'realistics' as button fanciers call them—buttons in the shape of objects such as fruit, lollipops, musical instruments, fish, and here, circus horses. Anything, in fact, so long as it didn't look like a button.

Elsa Schiaparelli's debut was by way of a hand-knitted sweater, featuring a white *trompe-l'oeil* bow on a black background. It was new, it was different, and it found its way into the pages of *Vogue* in 1927: 'Chic modern sweaters are, of course, triumphs of fitting, and this hand-knitted one from Schiaparelli is also a triumph of colour blending in which the black and the white are so interwoven as to become an artistic masterpiece.'

There was no doubt that the newcomer had style, and her style seems to have been, 'If you've got it, flaunt it', her recipe being a rich confection including a good measure of Poiret, a touch of Patou and a sprinkling of Vionnet. The rest was pure Elsa, and she was inclined to overdecorate in shocking pink (her favourite colour) with green sequins and metallic thread. The fashion press and the clientele, always seeking something novel and ever hopeful, found what they were looking for in Elsa, a seemingly endless source of ideas—something to talk about.

Schiaparelli totally changed the stately pace of couture, just as Poiret had done, and her clothes presaged the styles of today. She was the punk designer of the 1930s and always hovered on the brink of vulgarity and gaudiness. She lacked Chanel's enduring qualities of solid, functional elegance; Chanel, like Patou, was a traditional couturier, while Schiaparelli was an *arriviste* who took the world of couture by the scruff of the neck, shook it, and then produced for it a fresh, lively, irreverent look which was sorely needed to lift it out of the gloom of the Depression. The patient needed a restorative, and Elsa was the tonic.

A Schiaparelli design, following her penchant for trompe l'oeil *imagery, created in 1936 and photographed here by Cecil Beaton. American* Vogue *commented, 'As in prize-fighting, if you want to make a hit you must make it above the waist. Everything happens between the belt and the shoulders.'*

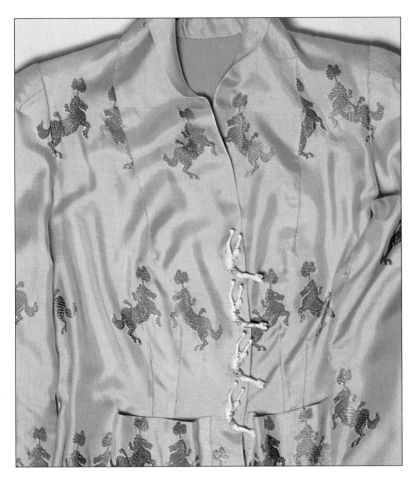

Schiaparelli's fondness for themes on which to base her collections produced this jacket of silk brocade from her Circus Collection. Decorated with circus horses and acrobat buttons, the fabric is dyed her favourite colour—pink. Her trademark was shocking pink, as this colour may have once been, but has probably faded over the years. About 1937.

At the start of her career, in 1927, Schiaparelli was designing and selling knitted sweaters and sportswear—often from a suitcase carried to buyers in hotel bedrooms. After being featured in *Vogue*, she took advertising space, and was picked out by *The New Yorker* and the influential *Women's Wear Daily*. Elsa was on her way. She designed bathing suits, wrap-around skirts, culottes, tweed suits, versatile scarves and knitted hats and berets. She began to give serious collections and to be taken seriously: the French actress Arletty left Lanvin for her. Daisy Fellowes quit Chanel, and Nancy Cunard deserted Patou.

Schiaparelli was evolving a personal style: a strict silhouette with masculine overtones, and decorated with elaborate trimmings. With her broad-shoulder or, as *Vogue* called it 'wooden soldier' silhouette, Schiaparelli did what Christian Dior was to do nearly two decades later, which is to confirm with total assurance and personal style, a tendency that had only previously been hinted at. She was not alone to perceive the trend. Marcel Rochas claimed to have created a wide shoulder in 1931: many couturiers would like to claim authorship of such a classic style.

Schiaparelli stunned the couture world with her inventiveness and audacity, appearing in a short jacket worn over an evening gown—it was revolutionary at the time. Her gowns sprouted cock feathers from the shoulders, or bore designs featuring handprints and, in one famous example, *trompe l'oeil* rips and tears in a white slim evening dress. She encouraged such artists as Cocteau and Bérard to apply their whimsical doodles to fabric designs, and used the freakish talents of Dali to design absurd hats (it was Dali who inspired the torn fabric motif) and gloves that bore the design of fingernails and veins.

It could be argued that Schiaparelli had poor taste and imposed her style upon the couture world by sheer force of personality and panache, relying on the maxim that you can fool some of the people some of the time. Yet her tweed ensembles, embroidered boleros and tailored suits are stylish and elegant and her wide-shouldered garments with a narrow waist were echoed in the mass-produced, everyday clothes of the late Thirties. She was one of the first to open a *pret-à-porter* shop (in the Place Vendôme) selling sweaters and skirts and accessories. She was certainly the first to employ zip-fasteners to couture clothes and make them a feature. The zip-fastener, by the way, was invented in 1891 by the American Whitcomb Judson, but the first practical zip did not appear until the Swedish engineer Gideon Sundback perfected the mechanism in 1913.

Schiaparelli introduced, to couture, coloured plastic zips, latex, cellophane, celluloid and glass fabric, horsehair, sharkskin, tent canvas and the wool from black sheep. Where other couturiers used buttons discreetly, Elsa's were used boldly, and they were unconventional in their appearance—shaped like animals, lollipops, padlocks, spoons, fish hooks and paper clips.

Sumptuous gowns—The age of clinging silk and satin

It was magnificent, but was it couture . . . or fancy dress? Many of Schiaparelli's clothes seem more in line with *prêt-à-porter* than couture, clothes that were designed not with one woman in mind (though Elsa promoted her own clothes, as Chanel had done, by wearing them herself), or even one type of woman from the Best Dressed List, but for a fantasy figure that was, after all, the creation of her personal view of art and design. Perhaps the source lies in her cultural past. As Palmer White says in the preface of his book, *Elsa Schiaparelli*, 'She was one of the rare designers to bring a background into fashion with her. This has to be understood.'

Considering her press coverage in the Thirties, especially in America, one might think that 'Schiap,' or 'Scap' as she came to be known, was the only couturier around. Yet couturiers practically fell out of the pages of French *Vogue*. By 1934, when American and British buyers had returned to Paris, *Vogue* featured Maggy Rouff, Robert Piguet, Chanel, Germaine Lecomte, Agnès Drecoll, Worth, Heim, Lanvin, Mainbocher, Augustabernard, Molyneux, Patou, Jenny, Andrebrun, Revillon, and Philippe & Gaston. *Vogue* even dared feature Chanel and Schiaparelli on the same page—perhaps they were short of space, so took the risk of inciting a riot.

At the collections evening gowns were a decided attraction. The Thirties was the age of clinging silk dresses that fell to the floor with a train. Every couturier featured them in his or her collections because they showed the couturiers' skill with luxurious fabrics and best expressed his inventiveness. In 1934 Molyneux showed Japanese-print fabrics with kimono lines and long trains, the fabrics a colourful display of Korean blossoms, wisteria, lilacs, poppies and hollyhocks, with bamboo buttons and accessories, Augustabernard created a graceful, evening gown of

Evening dress in bias-cut crêpe de Chine, about 1935 and rather muted for Schiaparelli. The fabric design is based on the motif of matches (detail ABOVE) which, along with cigarettes bearing lipstick traces, and cocktails for two, were typical themes of the Thirties in fashion as in popular song. Emphasis on floating elegance was achieved by the addition of long flying panels that could be worn over the shoulder or over the arm.

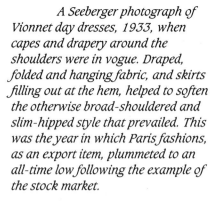

spiralling yellow chiffon. Vionnet's contribution was a pink satin affair with a square fronted *décolletage* and pleated sleeves, while Chanel had an ephemeral tulle dress traced with metal threads. Patou, true to form, had designed a slinky, black satin tea gown with a floating, pleated train shrouded by a cape of black tulle. For his *pièce de résistance*, Patou pulled out all the stops and showed a collection of gowns which, as *Vogue* reported, 'turn you into a spirited Diana—wings fly out from shoulder blades, volants soar from the hips, trains swish along the floor.' The Oohs! and Ahs! were finally concentrated on a sumptuous draped gown, later purchased by an American manufacturer in a moment of impetuosity. 'It was so beautiful,' he said, 'that I squandered all the francs I was supposed to spend on three collections on that one dress. When it was delivered I couldn't remember how it went on. It was a mass of folds and ends in the hand. I called my wife. She tried, but gave it up too. Finally we made something of it, but we'll never know whether we're right or wrong!'

The evening dresses of the Thirties were mostly of silk or satin, and silk crêpe or velvet. Often, they were bias-cut to follow the form of the body *à la Vionnet* and Grés and backless, down to

OPPOSITE: Trained, satin evening gown by Vionnet, photographed by Vogue's *chief photographer Horst P. Horst. Vionnet worked 'in the round' modelling and draping the fabric, first on wooden lay figures or dolls, then on the body, rounding the cloth to the shape and form, using her bias-cut technique, until she had created a veritable work of art of intricate and minutely stitched seams. 'When a woman smiles,' she said, 'the dress must smile with her.' This artistry is, of course, the essence of* haute couture, *and prompted Edna Woolman Chase to say that Vionnet was 'perhaps the only true creator in our time in the art of couture'.*

167

A Chanel ensemble, 1933, worn by Mme Quesnel. Dress, hat, shoes, and probably the jewellery and handbag, are from Chanel, the first designer to introduce the concept of the complete outfit.

RIGHT: Couture details of evening dresses: From left to right, a black sequinned trouser suit by Chanel, the jacket bearing sequins overlapping in the 'fish-scale' manner; dress by Mainbocher of gold sequins mounted on net; beaded, turquoise sheath dress, about 1932, by Norman Hartnell.

the base of the spine. Madame Grés, who in her first decade as a couturier worked under the name of Alix, was the designer of some truly awe-inspiring evening dresses, tea gowns and day dresses in the classical style of long, draped and pleated robes. She worked, like Chanel, on the live model, draping, pleating and pinning, using as much as 20 yards of silk jersey to make a practically seamless dress in a thousand incredibly fine pleats. Her timeless styles suited best the tall, leggy beauties of the period, such as Marlene Dietrich who was an Alix client. Dietrich had overtaken Crawford in 1934 as 'The Most Imitated Woman', which presumably attracted increased custom that Alix, in view of her painstaking methods, couldn't take on.

From editor to couturier — The House of Mainbocher

In 1933, and again in 1939, there was a curious Victorian revival which prompted Vionnet and, oddly enough, Schiaparelli to design dresses with bustles or large bows, sited at the point where the bare-backed evening dress plunged to the waist. The first revival was said to have been inspired by the costumes which Molyneux designed for the stage production of *The Barretts of Wimpole Street*. Since Elizabeth Barrett dressed in the 1840s, some thirty years before the late-Victorian bustle, the revival must have had some other source, unless Molyneux got his dates wrong.

These brief sorties into the past—there was a fad in 1935 for neat, three-cornered hats, *Directoire* hats they were called—show how some designers need a theme on which to base their collections, a historic or cultural ingredient. The Far East had been a well-tapped source for over eighty years; Africa, Egypt and the Arab world were similarly influential. Schiaparelli introduced a series of collections on music, Eskimos, parachutes and politics. She had the advantage in that she used practically anything as a source of design, drawing upon and exaggerating the nature of everyday artefacts, creating a vast reservoir of Pop Art that she made especially her own. 'A Schiaparelli customer doesn't need to worry about whether or not she is beautiful,' said a Schiaparelli customer, 'she is a type.'

By comparison the other leading couturiers of the Thirties, Molyneux and Mainbocher, were positively austere. By the middle of the decade Molyneux, who loved grey and muted colours, had formed a style of absolute simplicity, concentrating on tailored suits and pleated skirts. As for Mainbocher, he created fashions of such chaste simplicity that writer Sally Kirkland, in *Life Magazine*, said his fashions were 'underwhelming'.

Born in Chicago, Mainbocher began life as Main Rousseau Bocher (a French Huegenot name pronounced 'Bocker'), but out of admiration for couturiers Augustabernard and Louiseboulanger, he compressed his name to Mainbocher. He came to Paris and, as has been noted previously, became the fashion editor at *Vogue*, leaving in 1929 to found his own couture business, having made all the right contacts. 'Mainbocher, the former editor of French *Vogue*, has opened his dressmaking house in Paris, and his first models promise that it will be an important one,' reported American *Vogue* dutifully. *Vogue*'s view was not merely partisan, for Mainbocher's debut was impressive, showing luxurious and

The late Thirties brought in the pert hat worn well forward over permed curls. Dresses had higher hemlines, but shoulder pads stayed put. Dark suits were worn by most men (sometimes with a pullover underneath) and the fashion for the centre-parting (and judicious application of Brylcreem) came and went, and came back again.

inventive evening gowns of faille, the skirt sections being made of petal-shaped overlapping panels creating a sort of bouffant fullness to contrast with the short, straight tunic.

By the mid Thirties, Mainbocher had established himself and had built up a clientele including the peripatetic Daisy Fellowes, Lady Mendl and the Vicomtesse de Noailles. His most celebrated client was Wallis Simpson, the Duchess of Windsor to be, for whom Mainbocher designed the subsequently much-copied dress for her marriage to the Duke of Windsor in 1937. Made in blue-grey (Wallis Blue) crêpe, it had a high neck, a tight corselette waist and a floor length hem. The corselette waist was achieved by a small, pink foundation garment designed by Mainbocher and launched at his 1938 collections.

He was a resourceful couturier. He came up with the sleeveless day dress, since that was the way things were going (short sleeve dresses had appeared in 1936, the first time they had been seen for 135 years) and introduced the short evening dress and the strapless evening dress. Mainbocher's clothes continued the immaculate styles of Patou (who died in 1936, a year after Lucile). He produced simple, black dresses with high necklines, contrasting with beaded jackets and elegantly sequined evening jackets. 'High fashion is not for everyone' said Mainbocher, in reference to the more rarefied creations of couture. 'I don't think that most people want to be white blackbirds.'

For those who did there were more than enough couturiers to go around, couturiers who were designing clothes with impeccable tailoring and no expense spared. America's representatives in the fashion stakes were Mainbocher, Norman Norell, Charles James and Clare McCardell; Britain's were Molyneux and Norman Hartnell, Hardy Amies, Victor Stiebel and Peter Russell, with Digby Morton for Ireland. But in 1937 one of the most highly respected tailors in the history of couture arrived in Paris from Spain, and was soon to be featured in *Harper's Bazaar*. This was Cristobal Balenciaga, whose story really belongs to the 1950s, as does that of Jacques Fath who also started in 1937.

Towards a fuller skirt — The comeback of the crinoline

There was an attempt in 1939 to return to the recurring 35-year cycle when certain designers began to feature fuller skirts, hinting at a bell-shaped profile. The new profile was overdue by about five years and was short-lived when it finally came. Lanvin had kept skirts full since World War I; in 1937 both Schiaparelli and Norman Hartnell followed suit, Hartnell because he had been commissioned by George VI to design a dress for the Queen's state visit to France. The King rather fancied crinoline styles, so Hartnell obliged with a picture frock. Schiaparelli's dresses were part of her 'ballgown' style featured in her theme collection entitled 'Music'. Balenciaga and Molyneux attempted to revive the crinoline. *Vogue* said 'Crinolines bring to the London scene the ample sweep and porcelain femininity of an earlier age.'

Mainbocher surmised that a nipped-in waist — and his corselette — would be essential to the style, but the trend towards a fuller skirt was to be postponed until 1947 when Christian Dior launched his 'New Look'. The pressing attentions of the Third Reich and its apparent indifference to any fashions save black uniforms and brown shirts threatened the world of couture, if not the world of fashion. Before he quit Paris for New York in 1939, Mainbocher said, 'I do not believe that dressmaking is an art, but I do think that it is an important part of living.' French *Vogue* closed down, its files were buried in the Forest of Chantilly, and Schiaparelli followed Mainbocher to New York, flying out from Lisbon in 1940.

In Britain, Hardy Amies, Norman Hartnell, Edward Molyneux, Digby Morton, and Victor Stiebel (who had opened his couture house in London in 1932) designed clothes for the 1942 Utility collection sponsored by the Board of Trade, under the regulations imposed by wartime restrictions on fabric. Actually, the designs were attractive by virtue of their simplicity and restraint. It wasn't art, but in the 1940s it was an important part of the art of living.

The 'toy soldier' silhouette, championed by Schiaparelli — the slim-hipped, masculine and angular style of the mid 1930s. This dress was the mode for 1936, a no-nonsense, no-frills (apart from big bows, collars and revers) year that saw the release of the futuristic, H.G. Wells' film Things to Come. *And come they did.*

Chapter 10

A FITTING END
1940-1955

Fashions made a brave attempt at ignoring World War II, or at best triumphing over it. In America it was fairly easy as there was no shortage of fabric or designers. When the film star Veronica Lake wore her hair in a 'peek-a-boo' style, her long blond tresses falling over one eye and down to eight inches below the shoulder, a million or so blonds—and not a few brunettes—promptly copied her. As a precaution against catching their hair in the machinery, the girls working in factories and on the farms started the fashion for headscarves.

In Britain, fashions were utilitarian but by no means unimaginative, since several ready-to-wear designs had been created by such couturiers as Molyneux, Hartnell and Steibel. Women now wore slacks, and shoes with cork soles and wedge-shaped heels. Remarkably, couture fashions survived in Paris. Jacques Fath designed very short almost *risqué* skirts, and Piguet showed a strapless evening dress. Schiaparelli went to America, Chanel retired to Switzerland, but over sixty couture houses kept going. The great event of the post-war years was undoubtedly the New Look of Christian Dior. With Dior, French fashions regained their supremacy and couturiers their confidence. Well before his untimely death in 1957, Maison Dior had become, as *The New York Times* put it, 'the General Motors of Paris *haute couture*'.

Schiaparelli, Mainbocher, Molyneux, Lucille, Worth, Balenciaga and Fortuny have all shown that you don't have to be French to be a leading couturier, nor do you have to be a skilled tailor. As we have seen, Poiret could barely stitch a button, and the great Dior was hopeless with a pair of scissors in his hand. Would-be couturiers may be encouraged to hear that you don't even need to learn how to design! The ability to make a sketch, a *croquis*, of a dress is useful but not essential. Chanel was a demon with scissors and pins, but never picked up a pencil. 'I don't sell bits of paper,' she snapped. Lelong and Piguet were unable to cut *toiles*, nor could they sketch but, in common with the other couturiers, they knew a good thing when they saw it. They knew what was right for the time, and for the client, because they had an eye for colour, for proportion, detail and accessory, plus the indefinable quality of personal taste.

Some were indifferent businessmen but efficient administrators, employing people who had the particular skills that they, the couturiers, lacked. Thus Dior and Balmain first worked for Lelong and Piguet as designers, backed by a team of tailors and dressmakers. They all shared one other common factor, they worked in Paris—the only possible environment for the production of true French *haute couture*.

During the Occupation of Paris during World War II, the Nazis, thinking that the couture industry could just as easily flourish in Berlin, proposed to transplant every couturier, tailor, *premier*, bolt of cloth and button to Germany, but were dissuaded by the efforts of Lucien Lelong, then the head of the *Chambre Syndicale de la Haute Couture*, who pointed out that couture was manifestly French, and by its nature would be unable to survive in a city lacking elegance, culture and a suitably refined atmosphere.

Lelong didn't actually *say* that, of course, but the essence of his message was heeded. Perhaps the head of the *Chambre Syndicale* pointed out the value of retaining the couture industry for the benefit of the high-ranking officers of the *Wermacht* in Paris, who would purchase dresses for their German wives and French mistresses. That is, indeed, how the dress industry survived the war years, supplying couture dresses to the military and to the black market profiteers; a combination of Gallic guile and mutual self-interest kept couture in the Rue de la Paix, rather than the Kurfurstendam.

Although Mainbocher had hinted at the way fashions were heading when he showed models with a nipped-in waist in 1939, the style of the war years retained the 'wooden soldier' look that Schiaparelli had pioneered. The War did affect fashion in Britain when enforced economic measures influenced the clothes that we wore, although British *Vogue*, and the photo-news magazine *Picture Post*, were occasionally able to feature American and even Paris fashions. French *Vogue* and its younger sister *Jardin des Modes* had closed for the duration, but the American and British editions kept going.

British *Vogue* was reduced in size but not in spirit, and American *Vogue* appeared much the same as ever, showing the indigenous talents of Norman Norell, Clair McCardle, Charles James, and the prodigal Mainbocher, who opened his New York

Slim-fitting evening dress and jacket, a study in simple elegance by the great American couturier Mainbocher, from his first New York collection, after leaving Paris in 1939.

Couture detail: Lady's Utility suit, about 1942, designed for the Board of Trade by a London couturier, possibly Molyneux. As one would expect, the cut, tailoring and finish are of first-rate quality.

premises in 1941, where he attracted such clients as Gloria Vanderbilt, Mrs Winston Guest, and the beautiful, stately Mrs William Paley, also known—rather unsuitably—as 'Babe'. There seemed to be no clothing shortage in America, though Harry Yoxall, the managing director of British *Vogue*, writing from New York in 1943, said, 'In America you expect to find what you want, and don't; in England you don't even expect.'

Make do and mend—Fashion goes to war

In beleaguered Britain, couturiers organized by Norman Hartnell formed an action group in a bid to keep the fashion industry going, on the premise that even in wartime people like to be well dressed, and that good-looking styles help to maintain self-respect and morale. As the Incorporated Society of London Fashion Designers, the group co-operated with the Government on deciding clothing policies and, apart from designing uniforms, made a direct financial contribution to the war effort. Daisy Fellowes was elected president, and Margaret Havinden became chairman. Included among the ten members were Molyneux, Hardy Amies, Norman Hartnell, Victor Steibel and Digby Morton. Molyneux, working through the Blitz in Grosvenor Street, built up such a successful business that he was able to realize about £1,500,000 which he placed at the disposal of the Government to buy munitions. Couture, after all, was to have an impact on Berlin.

Britain's wartime fashions are probably unique in the history of Western costume. For the first time, legislation dictated women's fashions (I am not including the prohibitions brought about by sumptuary laws), since it was necessary to restrict production. Accordingly, the Board of Trade set up a Utility scheme in 1941 which proposed price and quality controls on civilian clothing, including the number of yards of cloth permitted for each garment (3½ yards), even to the number of buttons allocated. There were fixed maximum prices in the shops, and designers of Utility clothes had to use fabrics that conformed to certain standards. There was a set of fairly complicated rules governing the categories and purpose to which the cloth was to be used—for military uniforms, for hospital blankets, blackout material, and civilian clothes. Two thirds of all cloth manufactured had to be Utility. Clothes fashioned from non-Utility fabrics were better made and more expensive, and keenly sought after, but even these clothes were subject to the nation-wide rationing system.

Clothes rationing was controlled through the issue of clothing coupons—so many coupons per head per annum—and rationing persisted until 1952. This meant having to recycle last year's dresses, to 'Make Do and Mend' as the slogan went.

Austerity proved a challenge to inventiveness. 'If you can't afford a spring hat,' advised the fashion writers, 'twist a new one from a coloured scarf. A scarf can be made into turbans, snoods and fetching bonnets.' London's Utility collection, designed by such couturiers as Hardy Amies, Molyneux and Victor Steibel, created many elegant clothes that managed to combine sophistication with expedience, even though some carried titles like 'Board of Trade Pattern No. 6'. Fashion-conscious women could, however, buy gas mask bags in colours other than the regulation brown, and, for those who could afford the coupons, a dress designed by a leading Paris couturier such as Molyneux for a give-away price of under £3 (Board of Trade Pattern No. 4, now in the Victoria and Albert Museum) was a chance not to be missed. Anne Scott-James, writing in *Picture Post*, said, 'Personally, I'd gladly wear them in peace-time, let alone in war.'

The standard, non-couture dress of the 1940s was the shirt-dress with wide shoulders, fullness in the bodice, a natural waistline, and a just-below-the-knee hemline. Made of rayon linen, it cost you just under £2 from Harrods, and seven clothing coupons, while a suit from Dickens and Jones, in wool, might set you back £10 plus 18 coupons. Hair was long, but swept back and curled under to a shoulder-length bob, worn with a hat with a high crown, and perhaps a sombrero brim, tilted forward over one eye. Shoes were practical. 'No woman is going to spend five coupons on a pair of shoes that won't wear better than ever,' *Picture Post* readers were informed. The shoe industry was inspired to create styles that took advantage of scraps of material, off-cuts that would have previously been discarded, producing shoes of leather combined with snakeskin, and suede with lizard. Boots were popular because they were warm, and crêpe soles because they were hard-wearing and 'broken-glass-proof'.

The one fashion luxury that slipped through the net of rationing was the gift of nylon stockings. Nylons were a currency on a par with gold sovereigns (most women would have plumped

Celia Johnson in Noël Coward's Brief Encounter. *Although made during World War II, the film makes no obvious reference to war-time, but clothes had a certain military look, such as the officer-style hat, the square shoulders (emphasized by the wide lapels), the utilitarian appearance of her rather severe suit, and the prosaic shopping basket.*

for the nylons) and the supply was almost entirely due to the generosity of American GIs stationed in Britain, although some consignments found their way onto the black market. Nylons, and chocolate Hershey bars, were exchanged for hospitality, friendship, love, favours. Nylon, the fabric fibre, was invented in America by Dr Wallace Carothers and first marketed by Du Pont in 1938. Along with Terylene, introduced in 1941, nylon has been the most important—indeed revolutionary—discovery in the field of synthetic fabrics. Perhaps the sheer quality of the stockings and the uncertain supply created a disproportionate demand, giving nylon stockings a real mystique—a laddered stocking in the war years counted as a personal and domestic tragedy.

A striving for gaiety—The wartime collections

The need for practical clothes, epitomized by Churchill in his one-piece 'siren-suit'—a dark-blue battledress type of garment that contrasted oddly with his cigar—brought about fashions that were nonetheless stylish and enduring. Slacks were one, headscarves another. Trousers for women became acceptable provided they were worn with flat shoes and long jackets; fashion observers noted, 'Not many women outside Hollywood commit the sin of wearing slacks with high-heel shoes.'

As for headscarves, they became a prime status symbol and have remained fashionable for over forty years. Worn by the international élite, by the upper classes in Britain, and endorsed by Royalty, the approved scarves were and are silk squares by Hermés, Jacqmar, Dior and Yves Saint Laurent, carried around the strap of one's handbag, or worn with a knot tied under the chin. But they had started among the women working in munitions factories as the uniform of expedience.

The extraordinary ability of fashion to survive (and of couture fashions actually to flourish) at a time when armies were hurling themselves at each other across the globe is a measure of its essential independence and neutrality. It is a solemn fact that fashion shows, revelling in silks, satins and sequins, flounces, feathers and furs, were presented in 1943 in New York, London and Occupied Paris. In London, the non-Utility materials were sufficient to create a selection of couture dresses, and these were shown at afternoon fashion parades, while the city lay under a canopy of barrage balloons, and air-raid sirens periodically sent the population hurrying underground.

The press, somewhat bemused by this display of luxury in the face of austerity commented, 'Elaborate day dresses are being sold containing up to ten yards of fabric, every gown gloriously embroidered by hand, and fashion shows organized at which women sit for hours, watching furs and high fashion gowns parade past—often the same women, day after day.'

Meanwhile, in the Rue de la Paix, the couturiers that remained in Paris were able to put on shows for those who possessed the *carte de haute couture*, a permit which was given only to Germans and to some two thousand collaborators. Holders of the *carte* could purchase couture clothes that appeared in a fashion magazine called the *Album de la Mode Figaro*. There were pages of fashions, featuring evening gowns by Piguet, Patou and

Post-war optimism and the return of haute couture: a backless, black satin evening gown from Paquin, photographed by Seeberger. The nipped waist and flared skirt was to form the basis of things to come.

179

Maggy Rouff, dresses in black crêpe with ostrich-plume hats, furs with flared skirts, nipped-in waists, big muffs and hoods. Throughout the War, Schiaparelli, Grés and Balenciaga showed annual collections. Chanel, according to rumour, was living in the Ritz with a German officer, and had turned her back on her couture empire. Schiaparelli, now in New York, had entrusted her couture house to her *directrice*, Irene Dana, who was Finnish and therefore neutral, and able to maintain the house spirit and style. The newspaper *Comoedia*, as reported in Palmer White's book *Elsa Schiaparelli*, reviewed the collection of 1944 while the Allies were preparing for the Normandy Invasion, and reported, 'Everything is new, imaginative, amusing, original, sparkling. Each model possesses a secret, offers a discovery and charms by piquant seductiveness. The striving for gaiety is very likeable.'

Reports of civilian life in Germany, reports no doubt biased in favour of the Allies, suggested that men were wearing threadbare clothes made of milk-derived synthetics, the shoulders stuffed with paper. In August 1944 clothes were in such short supply that the issue of clothes coupons was stopped altogether in Germany, yet in Paris textiles were still available although limited; Grés and Balenciaga were ordered by the Germans to close their houses when it was discovered that they had exceeded the authorized yardage. They were reprieved for the autumn collections, when the other couture houses joined forces to help them get their dresses ready on time.

One couturier, however, was past caring. In 1944, Paul Poiret was dying of Parkinson's disease, heart failure, privation and exposure as a result of painting in the streets of Paris, minus a coat and in bitterly cold weather. His pictures were to make up his last collection, exhibited in March, and organized on his behalf by Segonzac, Cocteau, Derain and Villeboeuf. On April 28th, Poiret died. A year later, in the summer of 1945, a woman dressed in a black Poiret outfit, knelt by his grave in the Montmartre Cemetery. It was Elsa Schiaparelli, who had returned from New York, and had come to pay her respects to the man who had inspired and encouraged her. At least the old soldier received a medal, for Poiret was awarded *La Legion d'Honneur* in 1944.

The eye of the beholder—Fashion and the media

Schiaparelli and Poiret were two of the great entertainers of fashion, and, along with Patou and Dior, laid the foundations of our modern fashion scene—the razzmatazz style of presentation, the catwalk capers, the media hype. The media has had a profound influence on the way that fashions are marketed, and the fashion artists, editors and photographers have played a major role in shaping public attitudes. Right from the first popular fashion plates of the late eighteenth century, the aim of the artist has been simple: to show the dress in detail and at the same time create an appealing image (usually impossibly slim-waisted), a reflection of the feminine and masculine ideal.

The fashion artist, as we understand and recognize him today, began when Lucien Vogel founded the delightful (and now much collected) magazine *La Gazette du Bon Ton* in 1912. Vogel gathered a coterie of avant-garde illustrators such as Paul Iribe,

Couture collections held in Paris during the Occupation featured creations by Piguet (ABOVE), Maison Patou, and Maggy Rouff. The House of Schiaparelli kept going, though Elsa was making promotional tours of the United States to aid the war effort.

André Marty, and Georges Lepape, who were encouraged by Poiret and did much to popularize the Poiret style. By the 1920s, fashion reporting had become a branch of journalism in its own right, and artists created an entirely new style of graphic art, enhancing the pages of *Vogue*, *Harper's Bazaar*, *Femina* and *Jardin des Modes*.

Always on the look-out for new talent, the magazines vied with each other to snap up any artist that showed promise. Christian 'Bebe' Bérard was lured to *Vogue*, as were Cecil Beaton, René Willaumez, René Bouché and Carl Erikson. *Vogue* also grabbed the Spanish artist Eduardo Benito whose geometric, Art Deco drawings gave *Vogue* covers such style and impact during the 1930s. The Russian artist and designer Erté became the exclusive property of *Harper's Bazaar*, as were Marcel Vertés and Jacques Demachy.

The fashion artists, and the editors such as Carmel Snow and Diana Vreeland with their impeccable sense of style and

Evening dress in silk by Molyneux, 1945, designed after Molyneux's return to Paris and to his House in the Rue Royale. Here, he trained the young Marc Bohan, and gave him this advice: 'When you have designed clothes women are tempted by, then you have succeeded.'

timing, maintained high standards of presentation and reporting. They also directed the talents of the first prominent fashion photographers—the Seeberger brothers, Horst, and George Hoyningen-Huene, a Russian baron and *enfant terrible*, who repaid the interest of *Harper's* art director by tipping a plate of food into his lap during a 'working lunch'. One of the baron's protégés was the photographer Horst, a close confidant of Chanel, who worked for *Vogue*, along with Cecil Beaton. The supremacy of the fashion photograph over the fashion drawing is a fiercely-debated studio topic. The fashion artist can exaggerate, although there must always be a basis of truth, while the final image aims to convey, with wit and brevity, a feeling, a mood. Both the artist and the photographer induce the reader to identify with the image, but the camera can achieve this more easily since it shows the real dress on a real person. The fashion model, her style, her physical appearance and her chic, can have an immediate influence on an entire generation of women.

Of course, the camera *does* lie, and the art of retouching fashion photographs is almost as old as the genre itself. Horst photographed the remarkably beautiful Paulette Goddard for *Vogue*, in 1936, then retouched the print to trim the waist, slim down the hips, and remove laughter lines on the face. The skilful photographer, or artist, pounces on the salient features of a garment, understanding its construction, and appraising its 'message'. The venerable photographer Louise Dahl-Wolfe, who worked for *Harper's Bazaar* from 1936 until 1958, said, 'When I look at a photograph I can actually tell whether or not the clothes are well made. A good garment photographs well. It fits the body and has a special, entirely distinctive "look". Designers like Dior and Chanel were meticulous. Their clothes were as beautiful on the inside as on the outside.'

Chanel was to make her famous come-back in the 1950s, a period dominated by the immaculate, pure styles of Balenciaga and Balmain, and by one other couturier whose rise was meteoric and whose reign was sadly brief. While Lucian Lelong was persuading the Germans to keep couture in Paris, a middle-aged farm worker was growing melons and tomatoes on the Côte d'Azur. The grower was Christian Dior, keeping a low profile on his father's smallholding, before returning to Paris to join Lelong as a designer. He was to realize worldwide fame through just one fashion show in 1947, an unprecedented event in fashion history. Even people who couldn't tell a gore from a godet were alerted to the name of Dior and the 'New Look'.

The structural elegance of the master couturier Balenciaga. He and Dior were the greatest of the post-war designers. Balenciaga was, for Cecil Beaton, 'the last of the great couturiers', who, when working, chose to wear a humble porter's smoke, perhaps to remind himself that the simplest things are often the most enduring.

The winter of 1947 was the coldest that Europe had experienced for over forty years. In Paris, the fashion press had gathered for the Spring collections, and American *Vogue* reported, 'The cold stiffened the fingers and froze everything but ideas.' Molyneux and Schiaparelli were back, and had both shown collections in 1945, when Pierre Balmain had decided to go it alone and open his own dress house. Wide shoulders were still in fashion, but Piguet and Lelong were showing suits with tight waists, more pronounced basques, and a longer, fuller skirt that proclaimed a new trend. American *Vogue* noticed that hips were emphasized, heralding a return to the curves of romanticism.

The main talking point in the *Bar des Théâtres* in the Avenue Montaigne where journalists and photographers gathered to gossip, was the new couturier, Dior, who had just opened his house along the Avenue. It was newly decorated, and Dior had recruited Marguerite Carré, who had been the *premier* at Patou, and Mainbocher's head saleswoman Suzanne Beguin. Christian Dior, like Patou, came from Normandy (Patou's family were in leather, Dior's in chemical fertilizers). Dior had the exceptional advantage of being backed by the textile magnate Marcel Boussac, who had clearly seen that couture had great commercial potential, if skilfully launched and marketed. A successful couture style depends, first, on the designer, and second on astute financing, and, if the designer has limitless resources, the recipe is fairly foolproof, provided, of course, that the designer can come up with the goods.

Before the 1960s, a fashion show in one of the big couture houses was a rather formal affair, sometimes exciting and with a charged atmosphere, but presented in a fairly traditional way. The fashion press and the buyers sat on spindly, gold chairs, surrounded by gilded mirrors, heavy curtains, chandeliers and potted palms. The models would parade, one by one, at a leisurely pace down the catwalk. Each would turn at the end, walk half-way along, take off her jacket, if she was wearing one, to show the entire garment underneath, pause to enable a fashion editor to reach out and finger the fabric, and return to the dressing room where the couturier and a *premier* would be waiting to fit her into the next dress.

Dresses in the collection were numbered, and a *vendeuse* would call out the *numéro* as the girl appeared. The collection always started with day clothes—suits, coats, afternoon dresses— then evening dresses, followed by grand ballgowns and finally, the *pièce de résistance*, the wedding dress. The show might last two hours, and in the dressing room all would be mad confusion (although not at Balenciaga's). If the dress was complicated to fit (as it would be at Balmain's with his elaborate ballgowns) the sequence might be upset and dresses would rarely appear in consecutive order. A round of applause would greet a particularly attractive dress or an innovation, cigarettes smouldered in tall, chromium ashtrays, slim gold pencils flew over spiral-bound notebooks.

'Deeply feminine'—Dior's New Look

Dior's Spring show was a record-shattering success where the *vendeuse* was obliged to shout over the prolonged applause. Bettina Ballard, American *Vogue's* Paris correspondent, who had spotted the newcomer's promise when he was designing for Lelong, said, 'I was conscious of an electric tension that I had never before felt in the couture. Suddenly all the confusion subsided, everyone was seated, and there was a moment of hush that made my skin prickle.' Dior had master-minded the presentation, and had rehearsed the models with the patience and precision of a choreographer. 'The first girl came out, stepping fast, switching with a

Dior by Beaton. At the dinner to celebrate the launch of the New Look, Dior's friend Christian Bérard advised him to 'savour this moment of happiness well, for it is unique in your career. Never again will success come to you so easily, for tomorrow begins the anguish of living up to and, if possible, surpassing yourself.' Christian Dior surpassed himself, and many other couture designers, until his death in 1957.

provocative swinging movement, whirling in the close-packed room, knocking over ashtrays with the strong flare of her pleated skirt and bringing everyone to the edges of their seats. After a few more costumes had passed, all at the same exciting tempo, the audience knew that Dior had created a new look.'

The essence of Dior's New Look, which he called *La Ligne Corolle*, was the jacket and skirt called 'Bar'—the most popular and certainly the most famous outfit in modern couture history. The skirt was of pleated jersey crêpe in black, the jacket cream silk tussore. The skirt was long and full, worn over a layered petticoat, with an 18-inch-waist-indenting corset, or *guêpière*. The jacket was tightly fitting, with a flaring, padded basque that gave prominence to the hips. Worn with the suit was a natural straw, coolie-style hat, and Goya pumps or white leather court shoes. Jeanne Lanvin, who had died just a year before, would have loved it.

With petticoats, corsets and curves, with soft, rounded shoulders and flared skirts, Dior had both reinstated femininity and revitalized French couture in one fell swoop. The press was ecstatic. Said American *Vogue*, 'Things were done on a grand scale; the clothes were elegant, *built* for a woman's figure. Each model was constructed with a deep knowledge of dressmaking, to give you an exaggeratedly feminine figure, even if nature has not.' British *Vogue*, somewhat obscurely, reported the collection as being 'the Battle of the Marne of couture'. 'His house was newly decorated, his ideas fresh and put over with great authority, his clothes beautifully made, essentially Parisian, deeply feminine.'

After years of austerity, Dior's lavish and extravagant use of material (courtesy of Marcal Boussac) provoked the inevitable moralizing and puritanical comments from the public and politicians. The New Look was condemned in Britain as being frivolous, wasteful, immoral, anti-social. Some women disliked the waspie waist and longer skirts; in Lancashire, women led a strike against the New Look, demanding shorter frocks and shorter hours. Anne Edwards in the *Daily Express* thought that 'The ideal skirt should be like a good speech, long enough to cover the essential parts, and short enough to be interesting.'

Sir Stafford Cripps, then Chancellor of the Exchequer, criticized journalists for reporting such radical styles, yet the New Look was not all that radical. Corsets, petticoats and full, bouffant skirts had been seen before, but luxury and prodigality in day clothes—*that* was new. Dior's supporting stars in that memorable collection were dresses of black silk and tulle for evening wear, a strapless evening dress, and a tight-fitting (fit exemplifies the Dior style) coat with flaring pocket flaps over the hips.

By the time Dior employed Marc Bohan and Yves Saint Laurent, Maison Dior had become a substantial part of the Boussac empire, having launched Dior perfumes and Dior accessories. Dior's line had influenced the designs of other couturiers, and one London store sold 700 copies of Dior dresses in a fortnight.

Ernestine Carter, for *The Sunday Times*, said that Dior's was the art that conceals art. 'Dior will always have two unique distinctions: with one collection he had achieved an end to which all dress designers aspire, that of, overnight, making every

The now famous photograph by Willy Maywald of Dior's New Look outfit which he titled 'Bar'. It was the style that put couture fashion back where it belonged—in Paris—and Dior in the Hall of Fame. 'Yesterday unknown, today famous', said the press. This was the model that launched a thousand copies and imitations—nipped waist and flared basque—the return to femininity after the squared shoulders that had dominated fashion for 17 years.

185

woman wish she were naked with a cheque book; and to him must go the credit for re-establishing Paris as a fashion centre after the long hiatus of war.'

Dior's astonishing performance somewhat overshadowed other couturiers in the 1940s. Jacques Fath had opened in 1946. Fath's was a bravura style which somewhat matched his restless nature and highly charged social life. He started a ready-to-wear collection in 1948, aimed at the American market, and running contrary to the rather confining attitudes of traditional couture. Fath, a dashing, handsome, blond thirty-four, preferred the slender, linear fashions and introduced bright colours into the restrained atmosphere. Another much-respected couturier was Pierre Balmain, whose style quite contradicted his statement that a couturier's task was to dress women for everyday living, since his forte was superbly constructed ballgowns of an almost architectural form (Balmain had started his career as an architect) that were so firmly made as to be almost self-supporting.

'I shall dress thousands' — Commercialization and change

Haute couture is the product of a select few designers whose limited output, nonetheless, has a far-reaching effect on mainstream fashions — the ready-to-wear clothes sold from retail outlets. It is also the product of creative minds influenced by many different factors: by their own background and training, by the *zeitgeist*, by their personality, by financial backing, by the wealth of their clientele — a clientele also limited in number by physique; several of Mainbocher's sequined evening dresses are very long, having been designed for tall American women.

The clientele, the fashionable women of the *haut monde*, might wear a couture dress for one brief season before passing it down to less fortunate friends, or employees. The paradox of couture is that the style is ephemeral while the clothes themselves are made to last. As always, there are exceptions — the clothes of Chanel, Grés, Fortuny have enduring style.

In 1948, a bare year following the New Look, a contrasting line emerged, largely promoted by Jacques Fath. This was the pencil-slim dress which was also shown by Dior, Balenciaga and Schiaparelli. The 'arrow-narrow' silhouette went for a time with dresses that had floating panels to give an illusion of width, as though designers couldn't decide which way to go, and were afraid to commit themselves. Clearly, the bell-shaped cycle was going nowhere, and the tubular profile had reasserted itself. Even so, for some years to come the New Look would affect mainstream fashion, and flared skirts with bouncy petticoats were to be a regular feature of 1950s styles.

Dior created his high-waisted, flared A-line in 1955, Yves Saint Laurent his trapeze-line dress in 1958, with a wide skirt that fell from the shoulder line, while Balmain countered with his own pencil-slim, fitted dresses. Dior's favourite couturier, Molyneux, retired and closed his house in 1950. Couture, and fashion generally, seemed to be hedging its bets, uncertain of the direction, fearful of the future and waiting, perhaps, for a sign from the *zeitgeist*; Courrèges was to be the next catalyst, in 1964, but the story of the Sixties is outside the scope of this book.

Summer dress and picture hat in cotton, by Jacques Fath, 1949, from the Cecil Beaton Collection, and now in London's Victoria and Albert Museum. It was originally designed for Lady Alexandre Dacre. The skirt is a wrap-around which buttons on the back; the bodice has a stand-away neckline, maintained by the stiffness of the material and the complex construction.

In America, couture fashions were by no means pale imitations of Paris styles, the leading designers being Mainbocher, Clare McCardle and Norman Norell. Norell, who as a young hopeful had been guided and trained by the American couturier and ready-to-wear manufacturer Hattie Carnegie, designed clothes that were described by Pierre Cardin as 'classic and serious'. They were also glamorous, as one would expect from a designer who had worked in Hollywood, in addition they were expensive and beautifully made. After Norell's death in 1972, his head tailor said, 'You didn't have to put a label on them; people recognized his clothes.'

Of all the couturiers, Balenciaga remained aloof, impassive, unapproachable (except to Carmel Snow who championed him in *Harper's Bazaar*), introspective. He sensed that couture, and fashion as a whole, was about to change irredeemably, and didn't like what he foresaw, or what he imagined was around the corner from the Avenue George V, where he had his couture establishment. Balenciaga could just as easily have become a monk. His personality would have suited the asceticism and discipline of retreat, and the purity of the black and white religious habit that has echoes in Balenciaga's restrained and formal style.

He retired in 1968, contemptuous of the commercialization of what was, to him, an art form. He reputedly closed the doors of his house for the last time, declaring, 'It's a dog's life . . .' But Balenciaga was also behind the times and, like Poiret, was unable or unwilling to adapt to needs conditioned by a faster lifestyle, rapid change and a younger, more informal élite. Chanel, though, had their measure.

When she reopened in the Rue Cambon in 1954, at the age of seventy-one, to a lukewarm reception from the press and those who recalled her wartime liaisons, she announced 'I am no longer interested in dressing a few hundred women, private clients; I shall dress thousands of women. But . . . a widely repeated fashion, seen everywhere, cheaply produced, must start from luxury.' Accordingly, she designed her famous suit, which was widely copied and indeed worn by thousands of women. Today, after what seems like thirty years of continuous revolution in fashion, couture is being reinstated. In a recent report, *The Observer* newspaper said, 'Like their frothy jewelled trains swooshing from thigh-high sheath dresses, the Parisian couturiers, rejuvenated by Christian Lacroix, have left behind them a new interest in made-to-measure clothes. Brash, upfront

Norman Hartnell's top model Dolores showing an evening dress at the Spring Collections in London, in 1953. This was the year of the Coronation when Hartnell was commissioned to redesign the Coronation robes, a prestigious task for the Queen's dress designer. It was the first time the style of robes had been changed since the reign of Queen Anne, in 1702.

glamour is the strict dress code set by the French at the recent *haute couture* collections.' Brash, upfront glamour! Balenciaga's worst fears have been realized. Yet brashness and glamour are in the very nature of fashion. Poiret could be brash, so could Schiaparelli. Lucile was glamorous, so was Molyneux, Hartnell, Balmain, Dior and Norell. Fashion is in a constant state of flux, and Norell bowed to the inevitable when he said, of the changes brought about by Courrèges, 'I'm sure that there are lots more people who made beautiful clothes. But that's not the point. What matters is who changed fashion.'

The great architects of modern fashion each have their claim to be pre-eminent. Some would choose Balenciaga, others Chanel, or Dior, Poiret or Schiaparelli. Diana Vreeland, the almost legendary editor of American *Vogue*, chose Madeliene Vionnet. 'She was without doubt the most important dressmaker of the twentieth century.' But Vionnet was modest about her achievements, and said to Vreeland, 'I never saw fashion. I don't know what fashion is. I just made the clothes I believe in.'

Dior sheath dress in navy blue wool — a favourite fabric and colour — photographed in Maison Dior, 1956. Ernestine Carter reminds us that in 1956 Dior 'came a cropper' when skirt hems began to rise and Dior attempted to bring them down. If anyone could afford to make mistakes, that person was Christian Dior.

PICTURE CREDITS

8/9 The Bridgeman Art Library
15 Glasgow Museums and Art Galleries
19 E.T. Archive
20, 21 Victoria and Albert Museum
26 The Bridgeman Art Library
27 BBC Hulton Picture Library
31, 32 The Wallace Collection
34 Fotomas Index, London
35 E.T. Archive
39 Private Collection
41 National Trust Photographic Library
47, 50 National Portrait Gallery
63 Mansell Collection
68 Courtesy of the Duke of Buccleuch
and Queensberry
70, 71 E.T. Archive
75 The British Museum
78, 80, 81, 82 E.T. Archive
83 Bulloz
84, 85, 86 E.T. Archive
91 Mansell Collection
92, 103, 106 Birmingham Museum and
Art Gallery
107, 111, 112 E.T. Archive
115 Collection, Musée de La Mode et du
Costume, Palais Galleria, Paris/photo
Jean-Loup Charmet
120 E.T. Archive
124, 125, 126 Collection U.F.A.C.
136 Birmingham Museum and Art
Gallery
137, 138, 139 E.T. Archive
141 BBC Hulton Picture Library
142 E.T. Archive
143 BBC Hulton Picture Library
144 E.T. Archive
145 BBC Hulton Picture Library
148 Sotheby's London
158 Victoria and Albert Museum
160, 162 Sotheby's London
166 Horst P. Horst/Musée Jacquemart-
Andre
167 Bibliotheque Nationale, Paris
168 E.T. Archive
177 National Film Archive
178 Seeberger/Collection U.F.A.C.
181 Collection U.F.A.C.
183 Cecil Beaton Photograph, Courtesy
of Sotheby's London
184 Willy Maywald © A.D.A.G.P.
187, 188, 189 BBC Hulton Picture
Library

Photographs by Piers Bizony and
Richard Vanspall are the copyright of
Dragon's World and appear on pages 1,
2–3, 6–7, 16–17, 22, 29, 36–7, 48, 49,
55, 56–7, 61, 76–7, 96–7, 116–7, 129,
130, 133, 134–5, 147, 152–3, 161,
163, 164, 165, 169, 170, 172–3, 175

Illustrations by John Woodcock on pages
7, 17, 37, 56, 76, 96, 106, 135, 153, 172
are the copyright of Dragon's World.

All additional material is privately owned
by Dragon's World.

A SELECTED BIBLIOGRAPHY

Adburgham, Alison, *Shops and Shopping 1810–1914*, Allen & Unwin, 1981.
Addison & Steele, *The Spectator*, Oxford University Press, 1965.
Baillén, Claude, *Chanel Solitaire*, Collins, 1973.
Baillio, J., *Vigée Le Brun*, Kimbell Art Museum, Fort Worth, 1982.
Baines, Barbara, *Fashion Revivals*, Batsford, 1981.
Beaton, Cecil, *The Glass of Fashion*, Weidenfeld & Nicholson, 1954.
Blum, Stella, *Victorian Fashions and Costumes from Harper's Bazar 1867–1898*, Dover, 1974.
Booth, Pat, *Master Photographers*, Macmillan, 1983.
Byrde, Penelope, *The Male Image*, Batsford, 1979.
Byrde, Penelope, *A Frivolous Distinction*, Bath City Council, 1980.
Carlyle, Thomas, *Sartor Resartus*, 1838.
Carter, Ernestine, *The Changing World of Fashion*, Weidenfeld & Nicholson, 1977.
Carter, Ernestine, *Magic Names of Fashion*, Weidenfeld & Nicholson, 1980.
Charles-Roux, Edmonde, *Chanel and Her World*, Weidenfeld & Nicholson, 1981.
Coleman, *Collector's Book of Dolls*, Robert Hale, 1976.
Corson, Richard, *Fashions in Hair*, Peter Owen, 1965.
Corson, Richard, *Fashions in Makeup*, Peter Owen, 1972.
Cunnington, C.W., *Why Women Wear Clothes*, Faber & Faber, 1941.
Cunnington, C.W. & P.E. and Charles Beard, *A Dictionary of English Costume 900–1900*, A & C Black, 1960.
Cunnington, C.W. & P.E., *A Handbook of Eighteenth Century English Costume*, Faber & Faber, 1972.
Cunnington, C.W. & P.E., *A Handbook of Nineteenth Century Costume*, Faber & Faber, 1970.
Dars, Christine, *A Fashion Parade*, Blond & Briggs, 1979.
Davidoff, Leonore, *The Best Circles*, Croom Helm, 1973.
Duff Gordon, Lady (Lucile), *Discretions and Indiscretions*, Jarrolds, 1932.
Etherinton-Smith, Meredith, *Patou*, Hutchinson, 1983.
Ewing, Elizabeth, *Fur in Dress*, Batsford, 1981.
Ewing, Elizabeth, *A History of 20th Century Fashion*, Batsford, 1974.
Foster, Vanda, *A Visual History of 19th Century Costume*, Batsford, 1984.
Ginsberg, Madeleine, et al, *Four Hundred Years of Fashion*, Victoria and Albert Museum/Collins, 1984.
Hesketh, Christian, *Tartans*, Weidenfeld & Nicholson, 1961.
Jarret, Derek, *England in the Age of Hogarth*, Hart Davis Macgibbon, 1974.
Jewkes, J., Sawers, D. and Stillerman, R., *The Sources of Invention*, Macmillan, 1969.
Keenan, Brigid, *The Women We Wanted to Look Like*, Macmillan, 1977.
Kennett, Frances, *The Collector's Book of Twentieth Century Fashion*, Granada, 1983.
Kennett, Frances, *Secrets of the Couturiers*, Orbis, 1984.
Laver, James, *A Concise History of Costume*, Thames & Hudson, 1969.
Lee, Sarah Tomerlin (Ed), *American Fashion*, Deutsch, 1976.
Lynam Ruth (Ed), *Paris Fashions*, Michael Joseph, 1972.
de Marly, Diana, *A History of Haute Couture*, Batsford, 1980.
de Marly, Diana, *Worth*, Elm Tree Books, 1980.
McClellan, Elizabeth, *A History of American Costume*, Tudor, 1937.
McDowell, Colin, *Directory of Twentieth Century Fashion*, Muller, 1984.
McKendrick, Brewer & Plumb, *The Birth of a Consumer Society*, Hutchinson, 1983.
Milbank, Caroline Rennolds, *Couture*, Thames & Hudson, 1985.
Mitford, Nancy, *Madame de Pompadour*, Penguin, 1958.
Moers, Ellen, *The Dandy*, Secker & Warburg, 1960.
Nunn, Joan, *Fashion in Costume 1200–1980*, The Herbert Press, 1984.
Pearson, Hesketh, *The Life of Oscar Wilde*, Methuen, 1946.
Pritchard, Mrs. Eric, *The Cult of Chiffon*, Grant Richards, 1902.
Raverat, Gwen, *Period Piece*, Faber & Faber, 1952.
Rhode, Eric, *A History of the Cinema*, Penguin, 1976.
Sadleir, Michael, *Blessington D'Orsay*, Constable, 1933.
Saunders, Edith, *The Age of Worth*, Longmans Green, 1954.
Squire, Geoffrey, *Dress, Art & Society*, Studio Vista, 1974.
Steele, Valerie, *Fashion & Eroticism*, Oxford University Press, 1985.
Swann, June, *Shoes*, Batsford, 1982.
Tisdall, E.E.P., *Mrs Duberley's Campaigns*, Jarrolds, 1963.
Thompson, Flora, *Lark Rise to Candleford*, Oxford University Press, 1954.
Walkeley, Christine & Foster, Vanda, *Crinolines & Crimping Irons*, Peter Owen, 1978.
Waugh, Norah, *Corsets & Crinolines*, Batsford, 1954.
Waugh, Norah, *The Cut of Women's Clothes 1600–1930*, Faber & Faber, 1968.
White, Florence, *A Fire in the Kitchen*, Dent, 1938.
White, Palmer, *Elsa Schiaparelli*, Aurum Press, 1986.
White, Palmer, *Poiret*, Studio Vista, 1973.
Wilcox, Ruth Turner, *Five Centuries of American Costume*, A & C Black, 1963.
Young, Agnes Brooks, *Recurring Cycles of Fashion 1760–1937*, Harper, 1937.

Belle Assemblée; Englishwoman's Domestic Magazine; La Gazette du Bon Ton; The Lady; Lady's Magazine; Life Magazine; La Nouvelle Mode; Picture Post; The Queen; Harper's Bazaar; Vanity Fair; Vogue

190

INDEX